Dance

AS THE SPIRIT MOVES

Dance

AS THE SPIRIT MOVES

*A Practical Guide
to Worship and Dance*

HEATHER CLARK

DESTINY IMAGE® PUBLISHERS, INC.

P.O. Box 310, Shippensburg, PA 17257-0310

"Speaking to the Purposes of God for this Generation and for the Generations to Come."

This book and all other Destiny Image, Revival Press, Mercy Place, Fresh Bread, Destiny Image Fiction, and Treasure House books are available at Christian bookstores and distributors worldwide.

For a U.S. bookstore nearest you, call 1-800-722-6774.
For more information on foreign distributors, call 717-532-3040.
Reach us on the Internet at www.destinyimage.com.

ISBN 10: 0-7684-2818-1
ISBN 13: 978-0-7684-2818-6

For Worldwide Distribution, Printed in the U.S.A.
1 2 3 4 5 6 7 8 9 10 11 / 13 12 11 10 09

Dedication

This book is dedicated to those who express with movement before the throne and capture His heart while doing so.

Endorsement

Since I first met King Jesus at age 16, dancing has always been one of the highest and holiest ways to encounter the very heart of Heaven. My friend, Heather Clark, has taken what too often is reserved for the gifted or chosen and made dance available to all who are created to worship before His throne. In Heaven, we will dance for eternity. Why wait? I recommend this book for those who worship in spirit and truth and express with movement His very heart on earth. Dance on Heather, and may you take a generation of holy worshipers with you!

Heidi Baker, PhD
Founding Director of Iris Ministries

Contents

CHAPTER 1

My Testimony

My Road to Salvation and My Creativity as a Child

Dancing is the thing I love to do the most. I love the abandonment of movement, using the body to create shapes, pictures, and emotions. For me, all other art forms—and I'm involved with many—are more indirect; they involve intellectual engagement that takes over my abandonment. However, dance allows me to express myself directly, without a filter. I am sure my level of expression has to do with the level of freedom that I feel in dance as opposed to other art forms. It's pretty unlikely that I'm suddenly going to let loose an amazing guitar solo, or paint

with passion and fury and end up liking it when it's finished. No doubt, freedom of expression has to do with the varying degrees of my gifts; for when I dance, I own my movements. I feel very free. Though I think I will always be able to grow in technique, for the most part I don't feel hindered by a lack of moves or lack of ability.

CHILDHOOD CREATIVITY

For five years, I taught and choreographed with no formal training in dance—though not by choice. As a child, I tried to take dance classes, but found myself wanting to create instead of follow. When the class did choreography, I always thought it should go this way or that way, and seldom seemed to agree with the choreographer. Instead of classes, I would spend hours each night practicing, doing exercises that I made up, choreographing, and finding out how I liked to move to music. Everything about dance was internal for me, not external. Everything has to start on the inside and then move outward, manifesting itself into a move. (Experience has taught me that this is not the case with most dancers.) I would find myself, even at school dances, off in a corner by myself doing interpretive dance to the songs.

I was a very creative kid. Growing up, I found myself at different points involved in almost every area of the arts. I used to love to come up with ideas that my sister and I could play: "Little House on the Prairie," "School," "Orphans." I always knew how the story could go, and my leadership gift would kick in. My poor sister, she wasn't even allowed to come up with her own lines when we would play. I always told her what to say. I know now that it had something to do with the directing gift that the Lord has put in me. Even as a child, I was exercising my creative foresight, and I knew how the story needed to go.

My main art form, however, was theatre. Before I was saved and the Lord changed my plans, I was going to go into theatre after graduating. I was involved in a few companies growing up and the stage was my passion.

After I was saved, a door
unlocked inside of me.

After I was saved a door unlocked inside of me. It was the doorway into the chamber of dance. I hadn't grown up in church, so I didn't know if it was right or wrong to dance, I just danced. When I got water baptized, I came up out of the water dancing all over. I danced in worship all the time, and I don't think I realized that everyone else wasn't dancing with me.

After being saved, just before my 18th birthday, I got involved in a local church that put on a huge production each Easter about the life and death of Christ. The director of this 200-member production asked me to choreograph the dance. So I began with 12 dancers. Those first months were very difficult. I was brand new at teaching, and the dancers were brand new at learning dance. That combination made for a frustrating few months. Partway through the production, I found myself complaining to the Lord. However, I felt Him ask me to continue with the dance group. Far from stopping, the whole thing grew. In fact, after the production, we went full force ahead, choreographing somewhere around 15 dances. We called malls, hospitals, and parks—anyone who would allow us to perform. We contacted the city to get a permit and went as a group to perform our dances right out in the streets of Kamloops! That was where the dance group was birthed.

For the first two years of dancing, I had never seen Christian dance anywhere else. I didn't know it even existed in other churches. I was being called upon to start dance groups in other churches, and in those early years we started some 20 groups in Canada, Finland, Estonia, and Guatemala. There was no example for us to follow. We were pioneering something down a road without a map.

So how did we learn? We would literally get together, pray, and ask God to teach us how to dance. We would spend a lot of time doing spontaneous dance and worship dance, and use the movements that came out of our spontaneity. Interestingly, in one session, one of the dancers felt that we should put pieces of material on sticks and dance with them. Remember, we had not at this point seen Christian dance anywhere else! So, off we went to the thrift store to buy *bed sheets*. We put the whole bed sheet on a stick and danced with it. We worked up all of our courage to go and dance at the front of the church with these enormous bed sheets. All three of us were going to go out together, just so that we could *cover* each other. We were so nervous. We lasted for about 30 seconds before our arms were exhausted. After that, we went to the fabric store for some lighter material! I felt the Lord call me to go to a conference, which I rarely did, and it was there where I saw dance for the first time. I was astonished. You can imagine how entirely shocked I was when I saw people dancing with material on sticks and in costumes. It all looked very similar to what God had taught us to do. I stood at the front of the room the whole time with my eyes wide open, trying to learn and absorb everything I could so that I could take this home and teach our team what I had just seen.

It didn't take us long to mature in our efforts. I joined an adult ballet class, but quickly found that my learning skills as an adult were no better than they had been as a child! I spent three months in my first ballet class, trying hard to endure, but I left every class crying in frustration and wanting to quit. It was only my stubborn nature that kept me there. I would watch the steps. I knew physically that I could do them, but my mind didn't know how to learn from the manner in which I was being taught—not to mention the fact that I was entirely intimidated by these experienced dancers in my class. After three months, I left that class and decided to go to another school where the instructors weren't so...uptight...I mean professional. That was when I met Gay, the owner of the Rainbow School of Dance, where I eventually taught. Something just clicked with me at that school. When I would take classes, she would say that she couldn't believe I hadn't taken any lessons. My natural gift was blossoming, as she was able to teach and encourage me in a way that caused me to learn. I gained a lot of confidence, and soon I was teaching figure skating and gymnastics as well.

Shortly after I started attending classes at the Rainbow School of Dance, Gay told me that she didn't really enjoy choreography, which was my strong gift. Consequently, the two of us planned the school's year-end show together. It was at that point she hired me as a choreographer. I was teaching the young kids, as well as the older. The experience forced me to learn ballet terms and a variety of dance styles. The next year I wrote the year-end show with 150 dancers. We performed a production called "The Pearl of Great Price," a show written from a prophetic word that I had been given concerning Gay.

THE PEARL OF GREAT PRICE

During that time, I had developed a performance/ worship dance group in our church called Dancing in the Gap. Together, we studied ballet, hip-hop, modern, and tap.

We performed together for conferences. We danced and used visual arts. In the process, we discovered creative paths to take both in worship and performance. This group was also involved in "The Pearl of Great Price" production. Pearl was a great time for me because I was able to do what I really love the most—productions. I really love choreography and directing. It was a change to really challenge myself with something that I hadn't done before, at least not in this capacity. Directing and choreographing were a great success. It started out as a prophetic word for Gay, the owner of the studio, and as it developed, there were lots of relationships that were built and many opportunities to share about the Lord. People received salvation through the show, and our whole team was greatly encouraged. During this time, I gained confidence in knowing that I really could go into the secular arena and have something to offer.

In some ways, these early years were very difficult. The dancers and I were very much alone and tested, but we managed to make it through these trying times. There were no mentors. There were no spiritual leaders pointing the way that we should walk. But I want to take a moment to say that my pastor, Rick Parkyn, may not have been able to mentor us in dance, but he did the next best thing. He provided a covering for us so that we could learn and make mistakes. He opened a door for us. He loved dance and wanted to see it become a regular part of the Church community. To this day, I still say that he is a very big reason we developed in dance in the first place.

Eventually, our team would be asked to dance for conferences, and we were invited to teach in a variety of different places. We challenged ourselves any way that we could.

Since that time we have gone on to do many different productions, including one of our most known, *Emotion*. *Emotion* is the true story of a young girl who loses her father to cancer and takes on the guilt and shame of her father's death. It develops the emotional state of the girl through the different stages of her life. She separates from her emotions because she can't deal with the way she feels. Later in the show, healing comes and she makes a choice to walk in wholeness. The show has a variety of dance styles but is mostly modern. It's very creative and the quality level is higher than a lot of things we have seen.

We have started a production company called Collective Productions that puts on a full-length show each year. This past year we went into some local schools with it and

found that it was a great success. The company is our ministry that reaches out to the lost. The members of the company aren't all saved and the people we perform for aren't either. This is one of the areas that most excites me. I love to do productions.

We also have a full-time dance and arts school that we have developed over the last three to four years. So in each area of dance (performance, worship, teaching, studying, mentoring), we are continuing to grow and move forward. As the past 12 years have gone by, I have grown in my passion for the arts and especially for dance. I have come to a deep place of commitment to my growth and to yours.

MY ROAD TO SALVATION

I didn't grow up in a Christian home. My parents divorced when I was in grade 5. I don't remember ever being specifically close to my dad but I was with my mom. Even in those early years, before they separated, I can see that there were creative gifts at work in me. Those gifts manifested themselves in my childhood innocence. I loved color, movement, music, and writing. I remember in school always being the one to come up with the ideas for Christmas concerts and things like that.

I am a bit of a contrast in character. In one sense, I am very creative and emotionally inspired; and yet I am a strong leader and administrator. Therefore, while I was coloring and creating in school, I was also trying to organize the kids on my block for our weekly competitions in running, crawling, jumping, etc. The kids would all come over at a certain time just to participate in activities that I had organized. I had folders on each of them and what races they would win. I also made prizes for the winners. Our front yard had cement blocks near the house, and I assigned each kid a block to start his or her race. So there was equally administration and creativity at work in me. Leadership came very naturally to me, and people seemed to follow.

Shortly after my parents separated, my mom got into a relationship with an alcoholic. He and I did not get along. We were both stubborn and had leadership qualities that didn't mesh. He was abusive in many ways: verbally, sexually, and physically. The situation was very difficult. My mom wasn't saved at the time and she was locked in her own web of dysfunction.

One Christmas when my dad called to wish us a Merry Christmas, my mom's boyfriend got on the phone and gave

my dad a piece of his mind. He made us get off the phone, sat us down and told us that he did not want our dad to have anything to do with us. He said that we had to choose either our mom or our dad, and whomever we chose, we couldn't see the other parent. I don't know why we listened to him and thought he had the power to follow through with such threats, but we just listened.

After a long day, my sister and I sat down and decided that it wasn't fair for either parent to not have a child; so since I got along less with my mom's boyfriend than my sister did, I would go and live with my dad, and she would stay with my mom. By the end of the holiday I moved. Though I did see my mom again, my sister never did see my dad.

*I thought life
was bad at my mom's
but it only got worse
at my dad's house.*

24

I thought life was bad at my mom's but it only got worse at my dad's house. I was in grade 7 by this time. My sister was in grade 4.

My dad had horses a little distance from town, and there was a cabin out there. His girlfriend didn't really like me. I don't know all the details as to why. It could have been jealousy or anything, but either way, her dislike for me was obvious. In all the time I lived there, I think she talked to me about 20 times, and those times were never pleasant. Because she disliked me, my dad avoided spending time with me. He and his girlfriend would live at their cabin, while I lived in the house in town. I wasn't allowed out without asking for permission, and I wasn't allowed to have people over. These were extremely lonely years. I could go for three months and not see my dad. The only time that he communicated with me was when I had done something wrong, such as not cleaning something properly. I began to hate myself, feeling like if the two people in this world who were supposed to love me didn't, then I must be unlovable.

I paint this sad picture for you because I want you to understand something. During the three and a half years that I lived alone in that house, something formed in me that was profoundly important to my creative life. With much free time on my hands and no one to talk to, I began to write. I wrote every day: poems, books, short stories, plays, anything I could write. By the time I graduated, I had written over 800 poems. It was through this medium that I became very self- aware and able to express myself. I felt so different from other kids my age. I didn't care about the things they did. Others were interested in dating, drinking, and partying, but I was worried I would not make it to my favorite field to write before the sun set.

I didn't care that I was different. I loved being creative and was addicted to expressing. In those years my wells deepened. There was a passion in me, and I thought about things that others my age weren't thinking about.

I was too young to really process the damage that was happening to me at home. I knew that I was unhappy but I didn't understand why. I wasn't being yelled at. I wasn't being sexually abused. I had food on the table and clothes to wear; so why was I so unhappy? I had no idea the effects that neglect and abandonment could have on a person.

By the time I was in grade 9, I was completely committed to myself as an artist. I didn't just write poems to journal, but I wrote because there was art inside of me that was forming and had to come out. The loneliness and pain of life helped drive me into that place.

It was at this time that I also developed a desire for theatre. I was in my first full-length play in grade 8 after being inspired by a company that came to my school. In grade 8, I decided what I wanted to pursue in life: acting.

My hatred for myself was increasing all the time. I became suicidal and developed an eating disorder. I knew that my issues with weight had little to do with weight and that I was inflicting harm upon myself for attention. I was desperately lonely.

In grade 9, my need for attention was met in some ways by two teachers who took an interest in me. The first one was my English teacher. She would read my writing and encourage me in my gifts. I know that she wasn't aware of the depths of pain that I was walking through at the time, but she was there in a way that I needed. I think she was important to my development as an artist because I needed someone to read what I was writing and be a gauge for me on the quality of the material.

One day after school, I was walking into her room to pick up a short story that I had written. Her face was serious and she didn't change her expression as I walked closer to her desk. My first thought was that she didn't like the story! I stood at the edge of her desk and she pushed a paper toward me. Handing me a pen she said, "Sign this piece of paper, 'cause one day it's going to be worth something!" I was shocked. I never did sign the paper, but because she believed in me, I believed in myself. That day in her office was a defining moment in my life. I have never forgotten it. For the rest of my high school years, I always sought the acceptance of my English teachers, and I had a new confidence in my creative abilities.

The other teacher that was important to me was my French teacher. In this case, it had little to do with creativity. Because it was her first year teaching and she was young, we really connected and developed a bit of a friendship. We spent time together outside the classroom, and the long, honest talks we had kept me from really diving into the depths of depression.

Three and a half years I lived with no parental input in my life. I saw my mom only at Christmas and sometimes in the summer. My relationship with my dad was non-existent. He and his girlfriend worked shift work so sometimes I would have to go home from school at lunch to have a meal with them. This was terribly awkward because his girlfriend refused to talk to me. I would stare at her across the table all the time looking for some sign that she might warm up to me. My father would come to me often and tell me to stop staring at her.

As my creativity opened up and more expression poured out, my pain grew deeper. My sense of worthlessness increased, and my aloneness pushed me into depression.

At the end of grade 9, I packed up my things and sat down for my first real conversation with my dad. I told him that he didn't need a daughter. He needed a maid. He said he was sorry for how things had been and I had to believe that he was sincere. I don't know why he was the way he was, but I was planning to find somewhere else to live. I didn't leave then, but a month or so later, I had one of the most devastating days of my life.

I had a babysitting job and I was there with the kids when I got a phone call from my dad.

"Do you want to go and live with your mother?" he asked me.

"No, I can't," I answered.

"Well you can't live here anymore; so have your bags packed and be out by tonight."

I was stunned, but part of me didn't care. At that point, I didn't want to be there. I was cutting myself regularly, was full of self-hatred and wanted to die. I knew something needed to change.

There is something about pain and creativity that seem to be linked. It seems that pain can be fuel for creativity. Many artists say that pain causes them to create. I think it's because there is something they have locked inside that not everyone around them knows about, so there's an inspiration to speak out and communicate that pain. In communicating it, the artist feels less lonely.

I don't remember where I went that night. I just know that I went out without saying goodbye to my dad and moved to another city with a friend and her family. I saw my dad only one time after that when I went to see him around graduation time. I don't even know where he lives anymore. He wants nothing to do with me.

Although grade 9 was full of loneliness and pain I can honestly say that it was my favorite high school year. I was very creative! Of the 800 poems I wrote before graduating,

I think about 50 percent of them were written that year. Even though I felt dead because of the deep depression that I was in, I also felt very alive because never in my life was I more connected creatively.

My grade 10 year was the worst of my high school years.

My grade 10 year was the worst of my high school years. I dove deep into depression, feeling ultimate rejection from both parents and knowing that no one wanted me. I gained 20 pounds and sometimes slept 17 hours a day. On weekends, I would go to bed on Friday night and get up only to eat and go to the bathroom. I never experienced anything like this. I would try to stay awake, but my body would not physically let me. My hair started falling out in clumps, and I finally thought that I should go to the doctor.

Unfortunately, when I went to the doctor he didn't know what to do for me, so he told me to come back if it got worse. I thought, *What? In a body bag!*

I wrote very little that year because I wasn't awake enough to do much. This depression lasted seven months. At the end of that year, my mom called and told me that she was breaking up with her boyfriend and that she wanted me to live with her. I told the family that I was living with that I was going to be leaving so they gave my room to someone else. Days later, my mom called back and said that she wasn't going to be breaking up with her boyfriend after all, so I couldn't come. I told her that I had already given up my room, but she said that I still could not come.

My rejection grew deeper.

I did go live with my mom for the next two years, and I began to walk uphill, out of the pit I had been in. For the first part of grade 11, I think I was doing better than I had been for years. I felt much better. I started working out, got in shape and felt alive. I was able to function much better.

The next two years were filled with some ups and downs. I had some times of being OK, but then I would dive into depression again. Halfway through grade 12, I reached the bottom again.

My sister started having fainting spells that were unexplainable. She had many medical tests to try to determine the problem, but the doctors could come up with nothing. After a few months of this, one doctor came to see her in the hospital and asked her if she had ever been abused. She fainted right there. Because of this knowledge, the authorities forced my mom to separate us from her boyfriend. My mom was also at the end of herself. She called out to the Lord, and gave her life over to Jesus.

My first reaction to this was not positive. I was angry with her and bitter. She was very aware that she had sinned against us many times over the years. She wanted to repent and make things right, but I was not willing to forgive her so easily.

During this time, I was doing more theatre than writing, though I still did a lot of that. I was involved in a few different productions with companies, and I had the honor of working with some very talented actors and directors. Still planning to pursue a life in the theatre, I was involved in every area that I could. I was writing plays and producing them through my school, and at the same time, I was involved in companies outside of school.

Many people had told me about Jesus, and some very loving Pentecostals had very practically loved my sister and me by having us over to their house on Christmas, buying us gifts, and really caring for us. They always said that I should repent. I didn't really understand, though, because I couldn't see things that I had done wrong in my life. I didn't drink. I didn't smoke. I had never done drugs or slept with anyone. The only thing that I could think of was that I swore. Therefore, because I didn't understand the idea of sin beyond those issues, I didn't really understand the concept of repentance. I had been to church before and even recited the sinner's prayer, but I was not saved. There was not a real revelation of Jesus Christ in my life.

One other important night, I was talking with my husband, Nolan (who was not my husband at the time), and I was expressing to him how I felt so negative about myself. He was suggesting that I give my life to Christ and that this was the answer for me. As I was talking, there was something so incredibly evil that I felt. I had voices screaming in my head telling me that I needed to end my life, right then and there. The more time went by, the more frantic I became that if I did not immediately heed to these voices, then it might not happen.

I asked Nolan to leave the house so he gathered his things and went to the front door. He stopped and looked at me.

"I can't move," he said. "My feet are stuck to the floor!"

After arguing with him over it for a bit, I told him he might as well come back in. We talked some more, and then I asked him to leave again. He tried, but gave me the same answer. His feet were stuck to the floor in the same spot. The Lord was not allowing him to leave.

The Lord was not allowing him to leave.

A panic came over me. You know, sometimes when you need deliverance from something and God comes to deliver you, you can think that you're not the one needing deliverance. The enemy will do anything he can to confuse situations to stop God's work from coming forward. I suddenly thought that Nolan was involved in a cult and that he was trying to get me to join in. I started screaming at

him, telling him to leave my house and that I never wanted to see him again.

The demons in my mind were screaming too, saying that I needed to die right then. There was a war in the heavens that night over my life. Nolan looked me right in the face and said to me, "Heather, you need Jesus!" As soon as he said that, a few things went through my head. I am sure it took only seconds, but it seemed like half an hour.

The first thought was fear. I knew beyond a shadow of a doubt something very evil was in that room. I was scared. The second was that I had always thought I would give any-thing to God except my poems. In the past, when I had said the sinner's prayer or had spiritual experiences, the deal was always the same: God could have me, but not my poems. Re-ally, what I was saying was that He could not have *me*.

The third thing that went through my mind was that if I wanted to die and someone wanted my life, then why not just live as though I died that night and give my life to Jesus. No one else had ever wanted me.

I had a vision of myself sitting at a big table with piles and piles of papers around me, all my poems. I picked up the papers and threw them in the air. In my heart I said,

"Here, they're Yours!" As I did that, I felt a warm substance come into me. It started at my feet and poured into me until my body was full.

Nolan didn't know what was happening because I didn't communicate any of this to him. He looked at me and said, "What just happened? You're glowing!"

In one moment, I was completely delivered and freed. I didn't have a process to work through. I didn't have things that I tried to hang onto or fight through. I *never* felt suicidal again. I never faced that battle. I didn't hate myself. I felt love for the first time, and the person I felt love for first was my mom.

It is hard to write about your past when the mistakes of other people have contributed to who you are today. Today, my mom is a godly person. She is the best grandmother to my kids, and she has repented for the things that she has done wrong. Sometimes when people hear my story, they think that my parents were terrible. What they did was terrible. It was wrong, but these were two unsaved people disconnected from God and with low moral conviction. It could have been anyone. All of us have done things that were evil in the sight of God.

My sister was saved the week following my salvation. The night I was saved, my mom's new boyfriend (now husband) was also saved. They are both now an active part of my family's life. God did a miracle in our lives, and I am ever thankful for it.

After I got saved there were a few creative transitions that happened. One of the things that shocked me was the lack of creative expression in the Church. I felt like God told me that I wouldn't be in theatre, at least not in the capacity that I had once expected. It was fine with me because the drama I was seeing in Church seemed so cheesy to me that I didn't want to be a part of it in that capacity.

I would try to write, but all my writing was trite, shallow, and lacked content. Therefore, I put that on the shelf for a while. There was no pain in my life. Literally none. I still had to learn how to draw from a different well for inspiration and creativity. I didn't know how to connect to the Spirit of God to allow Him to be my source. Sometimes we express from the depths of our soul and sometimes from our spirits; all that is a relevant and needed expression of art. I no longer could do either. I had to learn how to let God be the author of my creativity. Looking back now, I see that the Lord turned the volume knobs down in certain areas of the arts to allow others to come to the front. I wasn't writing as much, nor was I doing theatre, but I was about to step into two other areas of the arts that would be crucial to the call of God on my life—music and dance.

CHAPTER 2

Why Do We Dance?

Shall I awake from slothful sleep
To mix my words with fountains deep
To breathe again though air not be
Shall I wear my heart upon my sleeve
Shall I draw forth 'neath broken breast
The fairest drips with which I'm blessed
Need be I shall let whispers unfold
The secret concealed dreams I hold
Shall I let love and love let me
Entrust to hands pure honesty
Shall I arise though scarred my face

To stand and dance without a trace
Of fear

This is a poem that I wrote daring to come alive as an artist, take risks, and be vulnerable. For me, no matter how much pain I am in, there is always a place of safety within the chambers of dance where I feel safe. I dance because I can't go without it. I dance because no matter how I try to deny this passion that burns in me, there is no denying the very core of who I am. Everything makes me want to move. When I hear music, it creates an inner movement that then transfers to my body. However, it's not just with music. Colors create movement in me. When I see someone paint, there is a movement behind the artist's strokes that can be transferred into physical expression. Creation moves me. If I stare at a river or a tree swaying in the wind, something inside of me has to join in that dance. Even if I don't physically move, inside I am dancing.

Consider the following observations from thinkers and dancers:

Aristotle said that the purpose of dance is to "…represent men's character, as well as what they do and suffer."

John Weaver, an English ballet master, said, "Dancing is an elegant and regular movement, harmoniously composed of beautiful Attitudes, and contrasted graceful Posture of the Body and parts thereof."

Jean-George Noverre, the great French choreographer, said, "I think this art has remained in its infancy only because its effects have been limited, like those of fireworks designed simply to gratify the eyes. No one has suspected its power of speaking to the heart."

Martha Graham, one of the founders of modern dance, said, "Life today is a nervous, sharp, zigzag. That's what I aim for in my dances. The old ballet forms could not give it voice." (Note: Quotes found in World Encyclopedia of Contemporary Theatre by Don Rubin.)

There are a number of appropriate venues for dance; it has its place in religion, the military, and in the celebration of societal rites such as marriage.

Modern military marches and drilling procedures are likely descendants of tribal war and hunting dances. Through history, war dances using weapons and fighting movements were used to train soldiers, preparing them emotionally and spiritually for battle.

Socially, dance has always been used in expressions of celebration, courtship, recreation, and entertainment.

BIBLICAL DANCE

I have heard people say, "Oh, yes, I know that dance is biblical. David danced before the Lord" (see 2 Sam. 6:14). However, the Bible has many more references to dance than we generally recognize. There are more references in the Bible commanding us to dance than there are commanding us to clap our hands! It is ironic, in view of this fact, that handclapping is much more widely accepted in church circles than is dancing. (For examples, see Psalm 149:3; 150:4, and Ecclesiastes 3:4.)

In the Old Testament, when people danced it was frequently a sign of celebration. For example, Miriam and her maidens danced in celebration at God's overthrow of the Egyptian army (see Exod. 15:19-20). Frequently, dance was a sign of humility and complete spiritual surrender. It was evidence that the person was not holding anything back from God, surrendering even his or her body to be used in worship. Even now, as we step out and dance, there is a line that we must cross to allow ourselves to become that vulnerable.

*Dance is a spontaneous
result of a heart that
is full of joy, love, passion,
desire, or even pain.*

Dance is a spontaneous result of a heart that is full of joy, love, passion, desire, or even pain. Some may ask why a person feels the need to dance in worship, but for those who have a need to express worship in that way, they can't help but dance. Actually, for those moved to dance, the real mystery is that others can worship without it!

There is something that rises in the heart of a dancer, something that clapping and singing cannot fully express. As the dancer is obedient, and follows the desire to express worship in movement, there is a drawing closer to God that occurs. When a dancer is moved by the Spirit to step out, his or her eyes are totally fixed on Jesus; a beautiful intimacy results from this worshipful obedience. Every act of obedience to the Spirit of God creates a closer relationship

with God. Out of abandonment to the Spirit comes a depth of relationship.

We dance because we are in love with Jesus. We dance because the Bible tells us to. If dance has a place in human warfare, so does it in the Spirit. We dance to make war. We dance to celebrate the goodness of God. We dance to lament. We dance because we can't help it. And we dance to express outwardly what is going on inwardly. Dance is a manifestation of what is happening in our hearts toward God.

For your edification, here are the forms of dance mentioned from the time of Abraham to the time of Ezra:

1. Processions—These were conducted as processional marches, which included music and dance. In our own age, we have had a revival of this in the form of the annual "March for Jesus." See Second Samuel 6:14.

2. Festival dance—These were cultural and worshipful dances done at festivals. See Judges 21:19-21.

3. Celebratory dance—Dances of rejoicing probably included circle dances and group dances. See Exodus 15:20.

4. Dance for weddings—In Israel, there was no seam between society and faith; a celebration dance at a wedding was a celebration of something given by God.

5. Dance of victory—Victory has always led to street dances. Look at the celebrations following WW II! See First Samuel 18:6-7.

6. Dance of warfare—These were dances done by those going into a battle.

7. Dance of greeting for the victor. This was done by the closest female relative to the leader in Israel. This was done to greet the victor after winning a battle. We recall that Saul and David were greeted by celebratory singing by those making *merry*.

Today, as dancers, we have again begun responding to God's leading. We discover that movement can be used to demonstrate what is happening in the Spirit, to bring a visual demonstration of what God's people are singing or saying. In a congregational setting, dance can be used to dramatize and reinforce what worship, prayer, or Scripture is declaring.

Anthropologists and historians tell us that primitive man danced for three reasons: love, war, and harvest.

Is it not interesting that all three of these causes of dance have spiritual counterparts found in the Church? We are inspired by simple love for the Lord to dance our expressions of celebration, intimacy, adoration, and exaltation. Many of today's worship services are filled with such dances. People can be seen leaping, twirling, spinning, and even running to express their love for the Lord! This is the Lord's doing, and it is marvelous in our eyes!

As well, there are many people who have experienced times of intercession and prayer that have caused them to add a more physical element to their dance; these involve stomping, kicking, punching, or chopping movements in the air. These are not people shadow boxing, but those wrestling with darkness. Consider that the Lord often caused physical acts to produce spiritual results, both in the miraculous and in war. Consider that in Exodus 17:6 the Lord commanded Moses to strike the rock so that water might come out. On one occasion, Moses' outstretched arms toward Heaven brought victory to Joshua's army (see Exod. 17:9-12). In Second Kings 13, Elisha enjoined the King of Israel to smite arrows on the ground as emblems of the defeat of Israel's foes (see 2 Kings 13:18). There are many other examples that we read in the Bible.

The dance at harvest corresponds to the dance done in celebration of the spiritual harvest known as revival. When we see the lost coming into the Church, and God's power moving in dramatic ways, there is a high celebration of God's harvest that will and should come forth in dance.

Although dance was a form of worship for the Hebrews, it also had idolatrous forms, both in other nations and Israel itself. When Moses went up the mountain to receive the Ten Commandments, the Israelites were busy dancing around an idol at the bottom of the mountain (see Exod. 32). The fact is that in history dance was a part of worship, whether pure worship or idolatrous. One can sympathize with why dance was banned; for heathens used it to worship idols. Perhaps it was easier to simply ban the practice than to honor its proper use. If we study the Puritans of medieval England, we discover that they banned not only dance but theatre as well. Since the arts easily lend themselves to idolatry, we are not unsympathetic to these measures, but it is as though the baby was thrown out with the bath water!

However, people still had, and always will have, the desire to dance. When the Church forbade its use, dance simply became increasingly secular in nature. Social balls, folk dances, and even the start of ballet were all a result of humanity's desire to dance. During the Renaissance, there was not only a rebirth in the area of the arts, but also in the Church. Dance was one of the things that for a season resurfaced in worship services. Worship, which had become dry and monotonous, now was more vibrant and full of life. There was once again an allowance for a fuller expression of worship in public gatherings. Sadly, fear again shut it out after a short season of tolerance.

As we have seen, there were many types of dance in Israel. It helps us to better understand what dance meant to them culturally when we examine the meaning of the words that they used for dance, and also study those who were dance leaders in biblical times.

MIRIAM

Miriam was the first "dance minister" the Bible mentions. She was a prophet and she was a leader. She did the dance of greeting for the victor! "Then Miriam the prophetess, the sister of Aaron, took the timbrel in her

hand; and all the women went out after her with timbrels and with dances. And Miriam answered them:
'Sing to the Lord, for He has triumphed gloriously! The
horse and its rider he has thrown into the sea!'" (Exod.
15:20-21). The Israelites were in a peak time of celebration, for they had seen their God deliver them from the
Egyptians. Dance was a central part of that celebration.

1. Let us carefully consider this fact: Miriam was a
   prophetess and she was creative in the use of
   her prophetic gift. She sang her prophecy while
   dancing with her tambourine. Dance can be
   used again as it was by her, as a way of delivering a prophetic message.

2. Consider the prophetic significance for the
   Church in what Miriam did. The closest female relative of the victor led this dance of
   greeting for the victor. Moses was the leader of
   Israel, and therefore, it was Miriam's job to
   greet him in dance after such a great victory.
   This dance is specifically important to the
   Church today. More and more we are seeing a
   release of dance in the Body of Christ. The
   point is that we are the *Bride of Christ*; He is our

Victor. We are, collectively, the closest female relative to our Victor! As the return of Christ draws nearer, the Bride is going to step out more and more to greet her Victor!

3. Miriam was also the leader of this company of dancers. There are things that we can learn from the way she led. Dance groups should have leaders to bring the group together for corporate times of worship and to serve the church in their collective gift. Dance leaders should call the dancers into times where the whole team speaks together either to God or to the people.

4. Miriam was sensitive to what was happening at the time of the celebration. Just before she stepped out in her dance, the children of Israel were singing to the Lord about how strong and mighty He was as He delivered them. They were singing about the greatness and excellence of their God. It is written, "Miriam answered them," (see Exod. 15:21) which shows that she was participating in the celebration, and as was appropriate, she led

the dancers out, using dance and tambourines. She expanded on the song being sung. Dance leaders and teams today should still respond to and expand on what is being sung in the service. This doesn't always have to be done in the same manner Miriam did, but she is an example to us.

5. Miriam used a prop in her dance, a tambourine. As dancers, there are things that we can dance with to expand our expression such as flags, tambourines, swords, sticks, or any other creative tool, things which help to communicate what is in the heart of the dancer.

DAVID

David was a mighty man, both in battle and in worship. His heart beat for the purpose of worshiping and loving God. Nothing was too extravagant for David when he worshiped. His sacrifices were lavish, his songs (Psalms) intense and excruciatingly truthful, his dance utterly energetic and abandoned. David used every form of worship that he could employ to express his deep love for God.

This was a time of lavishly expressed worship.

In Second Samuel 6, as the Ark of the Covenant was brought into Jerusalem, there was a celebration, "And David and all the house of Israel played before the Lord on all manner of instruments made of fir wood, even on harps, and on psalteries, and on timbrels, and on cornets, and on cymbals," (2 Sam. 6:5 KJV). This was a time of lavishly expressed worship. Every six paces there was a sacrifice. Evidently, much preparation went into this worship. "And David danced before the Lord with all his might; and David was girded with a linen ephod..." (2 Sam. 6:14 KJV).

1. First of all, contrary to popular belief, David was not dancing without anything on. He was dancing stripped of his kingly garments. It was a sign of surrender before God. When Michal judged him she said, "How glorious was the king of Israel to day, who uncovered himself to day in the eyes of the handmaids of his servants, as one of the vain fellows

shamelessly uncovereth himself!" (2 Sam. 6:20 KJV). Michal was basically saying that David humiliated himself by doing what he did; but what David did was humble himself in the sight of man and God as he danced with all his might. The truth was that Michal, being David's wife, should have been down there dancing herself! Not only was she wrong in judging him, she was negligent in that she didn't participate in the celebration.

2. The king of Israel was not concerned with how dignified he looked in the eyes of those around him. He worshipped with abandonment and in the company of the whole congregation of Israel. He played instruments with them and danced along with them. David was a man after God's own heart. He cared for what God thought of him, and didn't regard the opinions of men. There was such joy in his heart as he brought the Ark back into Jerusalem! We can learn from his example. David was not concerned with what his worship looked like to men, but rather surrendered fully to the Lord in worship. So should we!

3. Consider also that although he was the leader of Israel, he led by example. Leaders should still lead by example and not by simply telling others what to do.

By examining the meaning of the Hebrew words used in the Old Testament, we can often arrive at a better understanding of what the people of those times experienced. The student of Scripture will be surprised to see how often dance was part of Israelite celebration and the variety of dance they employed. Dance, then as now, involved a much wider variety of movement and style than simply jumping up and down.

Psalm 30:11 says, "You...turned...my mourning into dancing." The Hebrew meaning for *dance* in that Scripture is "a round dance," which is a group dance done in a circular motion. Psalm 149:3 and 150:4 tell us to praise Him with the dance. These both have that same meaning, "a round dance." The visual significance of the circle here seems to be that God turns misfortune *around*.

The following meanings come from the Strong's Concordance:

CHUWL (#2342)

There are some Scriptures that use the word *rejoice* (*chuwl*) and have the meaning, "to spin around under the influence of any violent emotion, usually rejoice or fear, be glad, joy, to go around in a circle."

> *"I will rejoice in Your salvation"* (Psalm 9:14).

> *"But I have trusted in Your mercy; my heart shall rejoice in Your salvation"* (Psalm 13:5).

> *"Therefore my heart is glad, and my glory rejoices; my flesh also will rest in hope"* (Psalm 16:9).

See also Psalm 21:1; 31:7; 32:11; 35:9, plus 35 more references.

MACHOLAH (#4234)

In Exodus 15:20, when Miriam leads the women out, the word for *dance* is *macholah*—a company dance involving singing. It is the same meaning for the word *dance* when the women came out to greet David after killing the Philistine, singing, "Saul has slain his thousands and David his ten thousands," (1 Sam. 18:7). We see another example of this type of dance in Jeremiah 31:4: "And I will build you, and

you shall be rebuilt, O virgin of Israel! You shall again be adorned with your tambourines, and you shall go forth in the dances of those who rejoice." This, too, is a dance company: a group of dancers set apart for the purpose of ministry in dance. It is no stretch to think of at least some aspect of this prophecy as pointing to local church dance groups!

KARAR (#3769)

When David danced before the Lord, the word used is *karar*—"to dance, whirl, or move in a circle, to exult, leap, run." This dance denotes something very vibrant and expressive, full of joy and emotion. Today, we seem to think that the only acceptable celebratory dance is the "Pentecostal two-step," done with our eyes closed and in our seats. However, biblically, there is more to the expression of dance than that!

However, biblically, there is more to the expression of dance than that!

The list doesn't end there, here—briefly—are other words used for dance and their locations in Scripture:

OLD TESTAMENT—HEBREW

Rekad (#7540)—to stomp, to spring out wildly for joy, dance, leap, jump or skip (Ps. 29:6, 114:6, 1 Chron. 15:29).

Dalag—to spring or leap (2 Sam. 22:30, Ps. 18:29, Isa. 35:6, Songs of Sol. 2:8).

Chagag (#2287)—to move around in a circle, specifically march in a sacred procession, to observe a festival, to celebrate, idea of leaping, dancing a sacred dance, to reel to and fro (Lev. 23:41, Ps. 42:4, 1 Sam. 30:16).

Hiliykah—a walking procession or march, a caravan or company (Ps. 68:24-25).

Shuwr (#7981)—to sing as strolling along, minstrel, to turn, travel, strolling along with a song (Exod. 15:1, Ps.33:3, 137:3, 100:2, Jer. 20:13, Isa. 54:1, 1 Chron. 15:27).

Halal (#1984)—to make a show, to be clamorously foolish, to boast, to celebrate (Ps. 149: 3).

NEW TESTAMENT—GREEK

❖ *Agalliao (#21)*—to jump for joy, be exceedingly glad for joy, very much leaping.

(See Luke 1:14,44,47; 10:21—there are 12 more references.)

❖ *Hallomai (#242)*—to spring forth, to leap up (see Acts 3:8; 14:10).

❖ *Skirtao (#4640)*—to jump sympathetically, to move, leap for joy (Luke 6:23).

Any unbiased student will perceive that dance is an appropriate response to God! In the Bible, people danced before God. If we intend to return to a biblical model of worship, dance should frequently be an integral part.

Yet, today those who dance before the Lord do not do so because of correct theology. They do so for joy! We dance as a response to the presence of God. Anything that can be expressed in words can be augmented by motion. A full expression of worship cannot be limited at all times and seasons to spoken words. We should—perhaps we must—write, sing, compose, paint, and *dance*!

TAMBOURINES, FLAGS, RIBBONS, AND BANNERS

Today, many dancers have chosen to dance with tambourines, flags, ribbons, and banners. Since this is prevalent, I think it is wise to consider a few scriptural references to these activities. In fact, all of these were used in Bible times as an aid when dancing. Then, as now, they add expression by amplifying movement.

Here are some Scriptures that mention tambourines, some of which have been discussed earlier: Exodus 15:20, Judges 11:34, Psalm 68:25; 149:3; 150:4. Other words used for tambourine are *timbrel* and *drum*. Tambourines were used in preparation for warfare, when God called His people to battle. As dancers beat the tambourine, they are using that motion as a representation of intercession and warfare in the Spirit.

The words *banner* and *flag* are interchangeable. As Christians, we use the word *flag* or *ensign* for a plain piece of material on a stick that can be waved. A *banner* is generally something larger than a flag and decorated with some kind of inscription. Biblically, the words for banner and flag are sometimes translated "standard." This is significant because, as we are holding up a flag or banner, we are holding up a moral or spiritual standard as well. (The two meanings of *standard* are etymologically linked, coming from the Old French word *estandart*—meaning simply "to stand.") More importantly, one of the names that God employs to reveal Himself is *Jehovah Nissi*—"the Lord is my Banner," (see Exod. 17:15). Some other references to flags in Scripture are Psalm 60:4, Isaiah 13:2; 62:10 and Song of Solomon 2:4; 6:10.

Although none of these specifically refer to dance, some do refer to celebration. Song of Solomon 6:10 involves the man comparing his lady to an army. He says she is as awesome as an army with banners. This tells me two things. First, an army with banners is something awesome, something wonderful with which to be compared. The second is that armies had banners. In the history of war, the flag was waved to give the army the next command. If the commander of the army wanted the archers to go forward, the standard bearer would wave the appropriate flag and the archers would respond. So the banner or flag, along with the tambourine, was also used in war. In the Bible, God Himself raises a banner, and in raising it, draws people to Himself. At other times, He holds His banner over someone to speak something. For example, Song of Solomon 2:4 reveals, "He brought me to the banqueting house, and His banner over me is love."

> ## *As we lift up a banner, we are proclaiming a message.*

As we lift up a banner, we are proclaiming a message. Banners can be really simple or very elaborately decorated. Using a banner is another way of speaking in visual demonstration. For example, if a banner said, "Our God is a consuming fire" (Heb. 12:29), that banner could be held up at a certain point during a song to provide an exclamation point for a particular word or expression. It can inspire people to seek after the One they are singing about, drawing them, as Scripture says.

God made the world with colors. Light—something essential to God's nature—contains every color. Each color is significant. As we understand the meaning of colors, we

can use them to emphasize acts of worship. When a congregation understands these things, it becomes even more profitable because they appreciate the significance of what worshipers are doing.

The following meanings were taken from the Bible dictionary, history, society, and one (the color lime green) that I made up! These color associations are written into the world, as well as the Bible.

❖ Red–fire, war, love, the blood of Christ

❖ Yellow/gold–glory, Heaven

❖ Purple–royalty

❖ Light blue–Holy Spirit

❖ Dark blue–spiritual authority, water

❖ White–purity, holiness, wind

❖ Green–spiritual growth

❖ Wine color–new wine

❖ Peach/pink–heart of flesh

❖ Brown–humility

❖ Black–sin, mystery

❖ Lime green–revival

When worshipers hold aloft these colors, they are really holding up spiritual symbols of spiritual standards: for example, standards of spiritual growth (green), or of spiritual authority (blue). As we use different colors, we are speaking in symbols of different standards.

Tambourine ribbon colors bear the same significance. A cluster of colors can have a specific meaning as well. A string of ribbons running across the tambourine—black, brown, purple, red, orange, yellow, white—together speak of redemption. A rainbow string of ribbons speaks of covenant. A person's wedding colors speak of Christ being that person's first love. Lastly, a string of colors that have red, hot pink, orange, and yellow, speak of holy fire.

None of this is meant to limit. We should be as creative with our dance aids as we are with our dance itself! Ask God what kind of banner He would want you to use in your church!

AN OVERVIEW OF DANCE HISTORY

When we look through history at the development of dance styles, we see how society and the Church came to view and experience dance as they do today.

In Sixteenth-Century Europe, we find ballet looking much different than it does today. It was more common and less of a spectator event. The ballet was very inclusive of the crowd and existed to provide entertainment at social events such as weddings, gatherings, operas, and symphonies. During this time, dance was a supportive art form, giving fuller meaning to a social event or another art form. Seemingly, it was not something that existed on its own. The shape of the room in which dance was performed was different in the 16th century as well. The rooms looked like miniature stadiums in shape, and the dancers performed in the center. It was so involving of the crowd that at the end of the ballet there was something called a Grande Ballet in which all of the audience members joined in with the dancers on the stage in a grand finale.

During the 17th century, there came a greater separation between the audience and the dancers on stage. In this era, dance was employed to tell stories or convey a theme. It started to have its own identity, independent and not merely supportive of other events or artistic expressions. During this time, the American Puritans did everything they could do to stop dance.

The 18th century incorporated drama into dance, creating the first full-scale productions. Prior to this time, dancers wore masks that covered their faces, but it was during this era that the dancers removed the masks and explored the potential of facial expression and portrayal of character. Along with the development of production, came the first use of lighting and costumes. In the Church, there were groups that began to incorporate choreographed dance into their worship.

Before the 19th century, there was little place for the female dancer. This was not isolated to dance, of course. Women were not part of dramatic productions either. Men enacted female roles. Even in literature, most female authors wrote using male pseudonyms; else, their work would get little attention. However, it was through this century that the female dancer became popular. It was an era in which technique was emphasized and refined. Dancers pushed themselves to achieve high standards of technical perfection. Interestingly, in Western Europe, where dance had been flourishing and most popular through the previous centuries, there was now boredom with the art and a loss of public interest. Yet, at the same time there was a flourishing of ballet in Russia. One Russian choreographer, Michel

Fokine said, "The art of the older ballet turned its back on life and shut itself up in a narrow circle of traditions." Fokine and others desired to develop the creative side of the dance. Out of this impulse came the first appearance of modern dance. Popular choreographers were encouraged to diversify their expression, to study painting and create pictures of their own. If modern choreographers were going to stay on the forefront, they were going to have to come up with new creative ideas. Whether they were embracing the new creative influences on dance or not, the influences were there.

CHAPTER 3

The Dance Companies

Some churches have dance occurring throughout the congregation. In such a case, dance is not organized; no one has been set apart specifically as *the dancers*. There are different seasons that churches pass through. The following section is for those who have specific dancers set apart from the congregation and functioning as part of the worship team ministry.

WHAT DOES IT LOOK LIKE?

A dance ministry can have a variety of appearances. Each group needs to decide for itself what it is called to do.

Evangelism

A dance team can be used to minister within a community at different venues. The dance team might consider approaching malls, parks, hospitals, or homes for the elderly to seek out places where they can perform within the community. As well, dancers taking part in secular classes can do so as an outreach. This in turn can lead to performing with unbelievers at festivals, year-end shows or other similar events. I would suggest that a consecrated group, set aside for evangelism, is the best avenue because working with unsaved choreographers, you have to do the movements that they choose.

Worship

A worship team can be a group of dancers who just commits to dance amongst the congregation—mingling in the worship service—or it can be a group that works more closely with the worship team and shares the stage. The floor at the front of the church can also be set apart to bring the dancers together for a more collective dance. When my dance troupe, called Dancing in the Gap, dances for conferences or festivals, we are brought in to minister on the stage.

When not performing,
the dancers wait backstage
praying, worshiping....

For those of you who have not seen dance on the stage with musicians, let me explain what this looks like. Usually, the people putting on the conference either build us a separate stage on which to dance or they simply divide the stage the musicians are occupying and leave a portion for the dancers. Backstage, we have two suitcases of costumes that we lay out and use throughout the worship times in order to emphasize what we are expressing. These costumes range from very bright and vibrant ones used for the more celebratory dances, to soft, long, light-colored dresses used in the slower songs. As the worship goes on, we take turns on the stage, as various individuals feel specific unction that matches the moment. Sometimes there is just one dancer and at other times the entire group goes out. When not performing, the dancers wait backstage praying, worshiping, and waiting to hear where

the worship leader is heading so that they can quickly change and go out.

Worship leaders who are more used to having dancers accompany them give us a list of songs, and throughout the worship the leader will really work with the dancers to show the congregation a group step, or just move prophetically with them.

Performing Dancers

Performing dancers dance as a group or an individual dances for the congregation. The dance is prepared beforehand, and should have a message for the people. This is similar to someone performing a solo in song on an instrument before the congregation.

PERFORMANCE VERSUS WORSHIP

Performing solo is an excellent way to introduce the distinction between performance and worship. Because dance is so expressive and visually loud, often people mistake worship for performance. First of all, I want to say that there is nothing wrong with either. As dancers, there are two separate calls. The first is to minister to the Lord and the second is to minister to the people. It is not wrong to do a performance. However, putting dance on a stage in the middle of a worship service is not performance. Andrew Smith, a worship leader, recording artist, and music producer, says about leading worship that we are called to, "entertain the Lord." Let it be that we entertain Him with all of our gifts. Because many congregations are not used to having dance on the stage right in front of them as they are worshiping, it can be distracting for them, causing them to think that it must be a performance. However, over time this impression fades and dance becomes viewed in the same fashion as are the musicians who are on the stage. It is just a part of the leading of worship.

On another hand, it should not be viewed as wrong for the congregation to watch a dancer. Sometimes we have the erroneous idea that if the congregation is watching, they are not worshiping, but as we listen to the singer and he leads us into the presence of God, so we watch the dancer.

Because of that call to inspire worship, it is very important that the dancer's heart is full of worship as well. I place a high responsibility on the dancers to search their hearts before getting up on the stage to be sure that they are up there for the right reasons.

SPIRITUAL STANDARDS

The spiritual standards must be very high. I think it is important to note here that not everyone who comes to dance class is separated to dance on the worship team. You might have members of your dance class who are not ready to take on the responsibility of being in the ministry side, but you can still allow them to be a part of the classes, and when they are ready, then they can be placed on the team. In the Old Testament, when the musicians, singers, and dancers went forward in physical battle, it was similar to the spiritual battle that we engage in today. Each dancer must be prepared for the spiritual battle. When leading the people in worship, there is frequently a fight. There are walls that need to be broken down or new places to which worship must ascend. The dancers need to be sensitive and prepared for these facts.

There are many reasons for having high standards. First of all, whoever is placed in ministry is being endorsed. The statement being made, in effect, is that this person's lifestyle and character are worthy of emulation—do what this person does. It is an awesome and humbling place to stand. We need to say with Paul, "Be imitators of me as I am of Christ" (see 1 Cor. 11:1). As leaders, you must not put someone in place of ministry because that person is competent to perform the dance moves, but rather because he or she is both competent and acceptable examples of holiness, worship, and submission—off stage and on.

> *"Be imitators of me*
> *as I am of Christ."*

Another reason for maintaining high standards is that when you put people in a place of ministry they will have cultivated the character to handle it. You aren't doing individuals a favor placing them in a place where they will be subject to spiritual attack if they lack the character and experience to withstand the enemy. The Bible says, "don't let anyone look down on your youth but be an example" (see 1 Tim. 4:12). Examples we must be, on stage and off.

What does it mean to have high standards? Here are some very basic Christian lifestyle questions to ask: Is the dancer reading his or her Bible? Has he or she developed a

prayer and devotional life? Is he or she an example of worship when not dancing?

I also would like to issue this warning to dance leaders: It is easy to set high standards, but it is not always as easy to stick to them! Sometimes, as a leader you may have a temptation to make exceptions—don't! Consistency is very important.

One of the ways to watch over the group that God has put in your care is to be constant in prayer for them. Sometimes it's difficult to *make a call* on certain situations because frequently what you are really dealing with are heart attitudes. Are they dancing for the right reasons? I have told my dancers if I feel like God is telling me they are struggling in their hearts and so I will come to them and talk to them— individually. We then pray through whatever might be hindering them. If there is repentance and restoration, where these things are appropriate, I don't need to take the matter any further. If I don't see a fruit of repentance, and I still have a check inside warning me, I will go to the individual again. If still there is no change, then that person is removed from dancing for a season.

As I say these things, do you wonder how I dare to make such statements—such seeming judgments on others? Perhaps you do wonder. Many leaders have asked—so I know that this is a major problem—"How do you tell someone that they can't dance? Who are we to judge their hearts?"

This is one of the most difficult things that I have faced as a leader. Not always do the things in people's hearts manifest in outward sin. It's relatively obvious, if not particularly easy, that you must go to those involved in sexual sin and remove them from the team. However, pride is just as serious, and you as the anointed leader will discern it. It is part of the bundle of leadership. You may have nothing outward to give substance to what you discern.

In such a circumstance, you then ask yourself, *How do I go and confront something like this?* To make matters worse, often people won't know that pride is in them. When confronted, they deny it exists. I had a problem with dancers who told me they were fine, but I would have this huge flashing light in my spirit. I would find out later that I was right and that they were not really doing as well as they claimed and perhaps thought. So I have learned this: as the leader, God will give you discernment. God has placed you in leadership over your dancers; therefore, He has also anointed, called, and equipped you to be responsible for the group.

One way to avoid many headaches is not to release people into ministry quickly. Make it clear that they will be released when they are ready. The other thing is—as hard as it will be—you have to be strong and follow your discernment. You must strictly follow and enforce your rules and standards. Because I have had a problem with young people lying in the past, I have had to really rely on what I was feeling God was telling me about the individual dancers. All my dancers now know that if I have a check in my spirit and I have sincerely sought God about it, I have the authority to remove them from their position until I have peace again about their lives. Don't get the impression that this happens all the time—removal from the team is in an extreme case. However, no matter how talented a dancer is, his or her spiritual state is most important.

The dress of dancers should be appropriate and their attire very modest: no short shirts, no tight shirts, no short skirts, and no sleeveless shirts that will reveal anything. I do allow tank tops. Some are more modest, and thicker in the strap across the shoulder. All girls must wear a bra, and if the dancer has a large chest, she is required to wear a sturdy bra and a sports bra over top. A simple check that we do is lift our arms and see if there is any stomach that can be seen, and bend over to be sure that no one can see down the shirt. Wearing a body suit underneath your clothes is a good addition to any outfit. Leaders, you must make your team stick to this. If you think dancers' attire is questionable, tell them they can't dance. I have had to go to some girls right before the service and tell them that they could not dance because they weren't dressed appropriately. That is hard sometimes, but it has to be done. Before the service, take a quick look at people to see that they are dressed properly. This doesn't mean that they need to wear dresses or clothes so baggy that you missed the person and the dance move in the clothing.

The spiritual state of your dancers is the most important area of focus. Lead by example, and have high standards. Some people may think that I am too strict with the standards that I have, but when you are doing something like dance that is somewhat controversial, highly visible, and so easily criticized, I don't think you can set your standards too high.

Lead by example,
and have high standards.

Dancers should not be released to minister in church until there is sufficient fruit in their lives. Dancers should be released for worship team service only after the following criteria are met:

1. There has been a significant amount of the fruit of the Spirit in their life (see Gal. 5:22).

2. They have learned to be sensitive to the Holy Spirit's leading.

3. They have learned that their ministry is to God.

4. There is nothing in their hearts that is performance-based or seeking attention.

5. There is a deep enough level of personal freedom in their lives in the area of dance.

6. There is a submissive spirit in them and they are able to work in unity.

Without these things, it would be premature to release dancers onto the team.

Why should a leader consider separating certain dancers from the rest of the congregation? When empowered by God, these are dancers set apart to minister the visual demonstration of what is happening in the spirit. The worship leader can call on them for a certain purpose. Some worship leaders who really respect the dance will actually incorporate it into their worship time. For example, if the worship team is having a hard time pressing in one Sunday, they can call on the dancers to intercede in dance. Dancers were part of God's original worship team plan in the Old Testament. There is power when the musicians, singers, and dancers work together.

How can worship leaders involve the dancers?

Some worship leaders are not used to having dancers work with them and therefore have no idea how to incorporate dance into worship or even make room for it. For a dancer, a worship leader can make all the difference in the world. At one event, we were asked to dance, but when we got there we found out that the worship leader for the event didn't believe in dance being used in worship—and

certainly not on stage! He felt that it was too showy and distracting. After discussing it with the leadership of the conference, they concluded that they brought us in to dance
and so we would do that—dance. The worship leader,
though, wanted to be sure that we were only on the side of
the stage and not at the front. That was a tough weekend
for us. We had to get up there beside this worship leader for
all the sessions and try to be free, knowing how he felt. This
was hard, especially when we had come to serve, only to
discover that the worship leader didn't care if we danced
and would have preferred that we not be on stage. Dancers
may overcome such challenges by talking ahead of time to
the leadership of the service or event, talking directly with
the worship leader to get an idea of how to work together,
or maybe taking the session off.

On the other hand, a worship leader who loves dance
can positively affect the dancing to a great degree. In my
experience, I would have to say that worship leaders and
recording artists Andrew Smith and David Ruis, fathers of
modern day worship, are the easiest and most fun for
dancers to work with. Working with them, one feels like
part of the team. The dancers feel free, for we know that
we are totally accepted and released to do what is on our

hearts. There's nothing like the feeling I get when I am dancing and I look over at one of them, knowing that both of us are saying the same thing by different creative means. Such an experience actually releases dancers to be more expressive and free.

Also, I know that there are times when both of these worship leaders have recognized some kind of anointing on a dancer and have lengthened the song, repeated a chorus again, or simply lingered to actually give the dancer the opportunity to finish what she was expressing.

Honoring the gift releases the gift.

I remember one occasion when David and Andrew were co-leading and three dancers were dancing. I was exhausted but decided that instead of leaving the stage I would just crouch down at the back of the stage to catch my breath and continue dancing. In this case, the dance stage was directly in front of the music stage, a step lower. I was huddled there not longer than 10 seconds, and Andrew came over to ask me if I was okay. I guess he thought I had hurt myself. His concern made me feel essential—a part of the big picture.

Worship leaders who make the effort to know their dancers, taking time to discover what's in their hearts, and why they do the things they do, begin to bridge the gap between the musicians and the dancers. Worship leaders can actually think of ways to use the dance, such as choosing a song and asking them to do something specific during it. Another way to bridge the gap is to dance choreographed dances with the band playing the song live. That too begins to erase the separation. Some songwriters are such a blast to choreograph to because they get so into it themselves.

A WORD TO LEADERS

Whatever you carry will flow down to the rest of the group. Whatever your life is filled with, those under you will pick up and manifest in their lives. I am very jealous for the purity of what is put up on a stage or up at the front of the church because it is an example to younger people and it's being offered up to God. As a leader, you are duplicating yourself in others in many ways. The Bible says that when a student is fully taught he becomes like his teacher. Paul said to Timothy, "Follow me in as much as I follow Christ" (see 1 Cor. 11:1). If you are a leader, others will follow you; follow Christ so that those under you will do the same. Your attitudes will reproduce in others your attitudes, passions, vision, tendencies, and dance style.

In addition, there is a supernatural transference of gifts and anointing through the laying on of hands. In First Timothy 4:14, Paul tells us, "Do not neglect the gift that is in you, which was given to you by prophecy with the laying on of the hands of the eldership."

It is important that as a leader you keep your heart right before God, and that you are constantly checking your motives and heart attitudes. You are daily duplicating yourself. If your heart is submissive and humble, you will reproduce that in others—likewise, if you are proud and rebellious! Those whom you are teaching will most likely admire you and try to be like you. Unfortunately, there are times when you may not feel like being an example, but you need to remember that you have been called to do this and you need to act responsibly.

Since you are a dancer, it is fair to assume that you have the qualities typical of most artists. The artistic personality has certain weaknesses that you will have to fight. Some things to watch for in your life and deal with before God

are pride, manipulation of others, being controlled by your own emotions, fear, poor attitude, lack of submission, lack of personal freedom, and past emotional scarring. These are a few of the things that can hinder you as a leader—things that will eventually pass on to those under you, if you give them space.

> *Once you are sure that God*
> *has dealt with your heart, you*
> *need to lead the group into*
> *that same process.*

Once you are sure that God has dealt with your heart, you need to lead the group into that same process. Be sure that all your dancers know that they are dancing for the right reasons. Sometimes it may seem like a repetitive thing that you are doing, always going to them to see that their hearts are in a right place, but a right heart is the foundation for a dancer's walk. I have come across people who wanted to perform dance, but not worship in dance.

People are not ready to participate in worship leadership if they are performance oriented. Each dancer needs to first be a worshiper. If you put someone on stage before he or she is spiritually ready, then you teach that person to dance first for man and second for God. I realize there are exceptions to this rule. At times, I have had novice people do a choreographed group dance for the congregation as a special number on Sunday so that they can learn to get out of their comfort zones.

A right heart is also important because of the fact that dance is something that is being re-birthed in the Church and when presenting something new to the congregation you want to show forth pure vessels properly expressing Christ. This will leave less room for criticism and judgment by those who are watching.

Here are some of the practical questions that you can ask yourself and the members of your group—some of which I mentioned earlier:

- ❖ Are you doing daily devotions? Praying? Reading your Bible? Worshiping daily?

- ❖ Is there any sin in your life from which you know you need to repent?

❖ Are you hurting in some area of your life and in need of healing?

❖ Are you carrying grudges against others?

❖ Have you been hurt and offended by leadership?

❖ Do you have any major insecurity that could hinder your service to God?

I have seen in my own life that when I personally come into a new area of freedom, those under me will almost automatically walk in the same liberty. When God has done a work in a certain area of your life, you can lead and cover others in that same area. At the same time, I have had opinions about things that I have heard come out of the mouths of those under me that I know are not their own conclusion, but are a result of something I have said. That happens in a positive way and unfortunately in a negative way as well.

I am sure that many of you who are starting dance groups have little or no formal dance training. You must not feel intimidated by that. Consider these encouragements:

Faithful is He [who calls you, He] *also will do it* (1 Thessalonians 5:24 KJV).

[God will]...*make you complete in every good work to do His will, working in you what is well pleasing in His sight, through Jesus Christ"* (Hebrews 13:21).

I am convinced that whom God commissions, God equips. I taught dance and planted teams in many different places for years before I took a single lesson. God even allowed me to get three different secular jobs teaching various forms of dance—all without training! When I finally did start to take some ballet, I was amazed to find out that God Himself had taught our team to dance and that much of it was very similar to the moves I was being taught in my class. My teacher would always ask me, "Are you sure you haven't had any lessons?"

God spoke a prophetic word to me one Friday night while I was praying with a few of my friends. The word was that I was going to lead worship from the piano. At that time, I didn't know what a single note was on the piano, and I certainly didn't know how to play. Two weeks later, I led worship from the piano. I knew every major, minor, flat, and sharp chord. A month later, I did some traveling with a speaker and did special music from the piano with her. I *know* that God can supernaturally supply the abilities that you need to fulfill the call on your life.

When you are teaching, you need only be one step ahead of the class. Take things slowly, week by week. Pray and ask God what you should do.

The dancer who told me that we needed to take pieces of material and put them on sticks and dance with them like flags did so before any of us had ever seen Christian dance, and before we knew that dancing with flags was becoming a common thing in churches. Your vision and zeal are more important than your talent and ability. Remember that God has put you in leadership, but the enemy will want to discourage you and tell you that you have no talent and that you have nothing to offer. Walk by what you know God has called you to do, not by what you feel. The work that God has called you to is new in many churches, and therefore, it is easily attacked. Have a strong focus, and be determined to walk through the hard times. When you are teaching and you feel intimidated, remember that the class doesn't know that you are nervous. Be confident as you teach, and they will learn from you.

Each dance group needs a spiritual covering, someone who can pray for the group and for the leader. This person should be a proven warrior—someone who prays for the church when difficult times come. Ideally, this person should either be someone in the church who has a heart for dance, or a fellow leader in the church who feels that holding a spiritual covering over the group isn't too much for him or her to do. You as the teacher/leader are also a covering to the group.

There are many things that you walk through during your spiritual journey as a dancer. Some of these you should, and some you shouldn't, share with your dance troupe. For example, when you are just starting out, if there are some people in the congregation who have a hard time accepting dance, it might not be wise to let the whole team know that. Some dancers are trying to attain confidence in a new area; they need to be encouraged not discouraged.

One time a dancer told me that one of the worship leaders said he thought there was ugliness in the dancers and that they shouldn't be doing what they were doing. I talked to the pastor about it and he assured me that it was being worked through. The leadership was privately working with the worship leader on his negative attitudes and judgments. A few weeks later, that worship leader stepped down from leading. If I had gone to the dancers and told them about what had happened, I might have planted anger, fear, and uncertainty in them and left them vulnerable to bitterness

and divisive feelings. It was my job to cover them. Sometimes the flesh wants to rise up and express the offense, perhaps looking for strength in the agreement of others. You, as a leader, need to rise above such things; you must act maturely and cover your dancers.

One of the reasons that a congregation sometimes doesn't fully embrace dance is that they aren't educated. In fact, many may have been taught all their lives that dance doesn't belong in church. On the other hand, some leaders may be surprised to discover a wide open door in the church: people who are really excited about dance. That is awesome!

> *The average church*
> *struggles with the idea of*
> *dance in the Church.*

Nevertheless, the average church struggles with the idea of dance in the Church. Move very slowly with the congregation if they are having a hard time accepting the presence of dance. I would recommend that you begin by introducing dances that are very beautiful—ones that are slow and graceful. Use much wisdom in choosing the types of songs and dances you employ in the service. Expand the worship horizons of the congregation gradually, using more and more creative things. Try to avoid putting your team in a place where they will be strongly criticized. Remember, sometimes you are dealing with people who have been taught for generations that dance is sin. Move in love for the people and in sensitivity to your dancers.

Have your heart open to the people you are leading. Be a spiritual mother or father to them, not simply a teacher. Being in ministry of any kind should never be used for personal gain, or to prove your worth to others. You are not merely a dancer; you're first a servant. Care for your dancers in their struggles. They have a place of freedom to reach, but it's a process—both for you and for them! Place them ahead of your own needs. Don't leave the slow learners behind and run with those who are the swiftest. Try to find ways to blend the group, meeting the needs of both extremes. Those who learn more slowly often turn out to be your most faithful, committed dancers.

If you are a visionary person, you will probably have little difficulty thinking of venues and trips for your dancers. Vision is very important, but faithfulness is just as important. It is better to finish something than to start it. Finishing involves many hours of boring repetition; these must be invested if you want to see the desired end—good dancers! You will reap what you sow; therefore sow into the dancers hard work, discipline, and careful training. As you do so they will grow in their technical abilities.

I have been questioned in the past about my taking secular dance classes and being trained by non-believers. At one meeting I attended, some women refused to participate because they felt that if one needed to be trained in dance, then it wasn't of God. Is this consistent? Do different rules apply to dance? Do we stigmatize musicians who have formal training? Similarly, do we believe pastors should take no formal training in theology? Experience tells me that many people who lead us in ministry frequently have many years of training.

Of course, I would never say that in order to dance you must be trained. That is not true at all. Paul had received formal training as a speaker and thinker; Peter had not. Is either disqualified from ministry?

Sometimes there is a problem for those who lack training. They also lack a diverse supply of dance moves. As a result, the dancers feel as though they are doing the same thing over and over again, and the congregation may get the same impression. Again, consider the analogy of Peter and Paul. Peter recognized that Paul's ability to express himself eclipsed his own abilities. Therefore, he wrote in Second Peter 3:15-16, "[And count the forbearance] of our Lord is salvation; even as our beloved brother Paul...[wrote] according to the wisdom given unto him...speaking...of these things; in which are some things hard to be understood, which they that are unlearned and unstable wrest, as they do also the other scriptures" (KJV).

Taking some formal training might help to expand your dance repertoire. If you know only ten moves, then you have only ten moves with which to express all that God pours into you! The more you know, the more you can use and the more you can offer for God to anoint! I would encourage those who feel called to dance, not to be afraid of formal, secular training. Right now, there aren't many Christian teachers; here then is an opportunity—go to the world as a light! Take what is appropriate that your teachers offer, and leave what is not. Trained ministers of the Gospel employ the same selective process in their education. Not all that the world says is useless; Paul quoted the inspired poets of Greece on occasion. Did you know that a pagan poet first penned the words, "In him we live and move and have our being"? (Acts 17:28). We don't need to fear the world. We need to go and be a light in the darkness.

PRACTICAL STEPS IN ESTABLISHING A WORSHIP DANCE TEAM

The first thing you need to discover is whether or not your church would welcome and cover a dance group. This is really important. With strong leadership approval and covering, you will achieve far more than if the church is—at best—dubious about dance. Go and talk to the pastor. Find out what his heart is in the area. If you think he may have some questions, bring some material with you. If I may say so, bring this book! Most pastors won't really know much about dance because they haven't been exposed to it.

A second step is to find dancers. Obviously, without dancers you won't have a team. Are there people in your church who you know would be interested in dancing? Talk to them and see if they are willing to commit to a weekly practice day.

Third, establish the goal for your team. If you don't have definable goals you won't get anywhere. Do you want a team that is powerful in evangelism, missions, worship, church ministry, or church planting? If you want a group that is equally able in all these areas, then you will need to focus on all areas equally. You will discover that there are different seasons for your team; sometimes you will focus on choreography, sometimes worship. This is fine as long as a balance is kept and you steer toward your goals. Without worship times—within the dance group—the group won't grow in worship freedom, and they will dry up in that area. Without technical teaching times, your dancers will not progress. A balance of time spent in each area will ensure that you reach your goal in the end.

A balance of time spent
in each area will ensure

that you reach your
goal in the end.

Some of the following terms I will explain momentarily, but here is a typical one-hour dance class schedule:

- ❖ 6:00-6:15: a warm up including stretching, mirroring, balance.

- ❖ 6:15-6:30: teaching.

- ❖ 6:30-7:00: worship, choreography, or special project.

Here, then, is the explanation of the foregoing. At the beginning of each class there should be about 15 minutes spent on stretching, doing any kind of balance exercises, and mirroring. Mirroring is a process where members of the group face you and mimic exactly what you are doing. Start out with very simple arm moves one at a time and progress toward more difficult movements as the group matures. This is good exercise to release a flow in dancers— graceful transition from one movement to the next. It also fosters the unified spontaneity necessary in a group dance. For example, this exercise leaves the door open for you to involve your group in a spontaneous, unrehearsed accompaniment to a song being played in worship. No, you haven't choreographed it, but skilled dancers trained to mirror your moves will do wonders!

The teaching time will vary with each session. One week you might teach new jumps and the next week you might focus on a tambourine routine. Of course, depending on the size and interest of your group, you may have specialists in tambourine and so forth. In that case, you will have to divide according to what best meets the need of your situation.

Here are different topics and technical aspects in which any dance group will need some instruction:

1. New Jumps

2. New Spins

3. Footwork—This involves any exercise that helps them to learn to dance, not only with their hands and arms but also with their feet. They can isolate aspects of dance, limiting the movement to their feet for a certain amount of

time. You might want to introduce a piece chore-ographed by you that highlights foot movement.

4. Mirroring—Face the team and have them do exactly what you do using mostly arms. If you use your right arm, they use their left, just like in a mirror.

5. Intense Mirroring—This involves the same process only performed to music and using more elaborate maneuvers than simple arm movements.

6. Solo Dance—Here you have each dancer dance in front of the group alone for a minute or so. This is an excellent way to develop the confidence of the dancer and to overcome any discomfort involved in performing before others. It also allows them to appreciate one another's abilities and strengths.

7. Gymnastics—Do this only if the group is able to accept challenging maneuvers and you are knowledgeable in how to teach them. Some appropriate tumbling moves involve back handsprings, dive rolls, cartwheels, head-stands, handstands, and back walkovers.

8. Tambourine—It is best to incorporate tambourine into an already choreographed routine, previously mastered by the group.

9. Flag—Again, it is well to incorporate flags into an already choreographed routine previously mastered by the group. However, it is also good to have them just dance freely with flags in order for them to get used to the flag's movement and to adjust to how this activity impacts their own bodily movement.

10. Eight Counts—This is done to a fast song and needs to be choreographed before coming to class. It is done one move per beat of the song. The moves are choreographed in groups of eight. You could teach about three sets of eight to the class and then practice. This is good both for helping the dancers to remember moves and for causing them to think quickly on their feet.

11. Individual Choreography—Here, they are given time in class to develop choreography, either to a song or in order to create a combination built from various mastered movements. It is well to have students present their

finished choreographies to the class. This exercises creativity and confidence, as well as allowing students to discover their talents in this important area.

12. Creation—Dancers are given time to create their own dance moves, jumps, or spins. It is a creative exercise, but also introduces fresh moves to the group as a whole that can be incorporated into dances.

13. Doctrine—Time should be spent teaching about the biblical background of dance. Alternately, a devotional study could also take place at this time.

The second half of the class can involve either a continuation of teaching, a time of choreography, or a time of worship. When you have a time of choreography, you need to first pick a song and choreograph it; then that time in class would be used for teaching that particular dance. Worship should be done regularly. To prepare for this, you need either a worship tape or someone to lead worship for you. Encourage the dancers to use this class time to experiment with different things. This should be a safe place for them to enter in and dance. Watch for those who tend to lag, stand back, and stay in their comfort zones! Encourage them to step beyond their predefined borders.

Monthly Schedule

Each month, it is good to schedule an event that will keep your group focused on a goal that they have to reach. Depending on various factors, once a month may be too frequent for your group, but you must adjust this according to your team's collective needs. The following are some of the possible events that you might consider:

1. Evangelism—parks, stores, schools, hospitals, old folks' homes, special events going on in your area. You simply need to choose a few songs and choreograph them. Ask for permission where it is needed, then take your group! You will learn more and more each time you go concerning what you need to do to prepare for subsequent events.

2. Church Events—Dance as a special event in church, youth services, seniors' gatherings, or children's ministry.

3. Unity Event—an event that is planned just to draw your team closer together. Unity is really important for your team. This could be an event planned that is not centered around dance. We usually have sleepovers, go out for dinner, go bowling, etc.

4. Special Events—musical plays performed in dance; this might involve a special event done in or for the church that is longer than one song.

YEARLY SCHEDULE

1. After three months—At this point, you might find it necessary to split the class into two levels because there will come a natural split in the class, for some learn quickly and others need more time. Experience tells me that there will be a natural break after about three months. The splitting of the group might partially reflect the variety of ages in the group, as well as the spectrum of ability. There have been times when we have had up to five classes in order to accommodate the needs of all of our students. It can be harder for you, perhaps, but it will be

the best thing for the group in the end. You will need to have your eyes open for leadership potential, as you will need help in instructing a proliferation of classes by yourself.

2. After six months—Make an open invitation to other people in the church so that new people have the chance to join your group. After six months you will have a good base and it will be easy to add to it. You don't want to have a large group too early. They will grow faster if you start with a good base. As alluded to before, if someone is really starting to show strong positive leadership skills, then start to involve them working with you.

CHAPTER 4

Introducing Dance as Ministry

Introducing dance to the congregation helps to build rapport between the congregants and the dancers. Especially for churches that are unfamiliar with dance as ministry, it is pertinent to provide a solid foundation and environment in which to worship in freedom.

Here are some practical steps to introduce the art of dance:

1. Find out what the leadership wants.

2. Find out something that will be happening in an upcoming service (baby dedication, baptisms,

sermon), and find a song that would go with such a theme.

3. Choreograph a dance to it that has very simple movements, mostly arms and little floor movement.

4. Find something to wear that is ultra-conservative and modest.

5. Before performing the dance, read a Scripture on dance and explain what the dance means.

6. Do the dance.

7. Be very open to people's questions afterward.

8. Follow the same procedure a few more times, depending how the congregation seems to be adjusting.

9. Have a number on the team who are ready to dance in worship. Find outfits that are extremely modest and wear them for Sunday worship.

10. At the front, on the floor begin to step out individually facing the worship team.

11. Do this for a number of weeks just to get the people used to seeing you there.

12. After a while of this, try facing the people, moving it to the stage perhaps. All the while, remain very sensitive and full of explanation.

This is an extremely important part of what you will do as a dance team. There are two teams with which I'm familiar in Estonia. Both dance teams had problems being accepted by their congregations. They reaped the consequences of the methods that they used to introduce their dance and were rejected.

> *Introducing dance to*
> *the congregation helps*
> *to build rapport between*
> *the congregants and the dancers.*

In one case, one team just wasn't ready spiritually; they weren't sensitive enough to the congregation. The second team introduced their dance to the church using a choreographed dance that involved upbeat, flashy dance moves that were somewhat questionable. This was a team of young people. The dance would have been wonderful for evangelism, but it was actually inappropriate for a Sunday morning service.

As I mentioned earlier, begin with a carefully choreographed slow song, something very graceful and beautiful. This dance will set the standard in the hearts of the congregation. I am not suggesting that slow flowing dance is more spiritual, but it will be more acceptable to your congregation, being more soothing. You might consider using flags or ribbons. I would recommend that the song be something very worshipful. Focus on arm movement and make certain the song offers a clear—if interpretive—message. In this way, you will really minister to the congregation.

Women should wear long dresses, something that is flowing and beautiful. Once dance has been presented to the congregation, then you can begin to give it a more prominent place in worship.

I should note that the amount of care used is directly proportional to the comfort of the church. If a church is completely new to dance; they will likely have uncertainty in their hearts. In such a case, be very careful. I suggest you don't try to blow up the congregation with your first service! Certainly, don't do a lot of movement at first. Allow the congregation a season to get used to the idea of dance. Then, as you sense they are becoming more accepting, you can allow more freedom to your dancers.

None of this is said to cause paranoia. Be free but allow God to lead you. He knows where His people's hearts are and what they can handle. As the Lord said to the disciples in Matthew 24:45, "Who then is a faithful and wise servant, whom his master...[has set] over his household, to give them food in due season?"

Our team struggled to be free in worship for nearly a year. Our church was one that needed to be gradually led into an understanding of dance. Every Sunday we would go, ready to dance, and every Sunday we would leave discouraged because we didn't fully step out. We all said that at different times there was such an intense fire burning in our stomachs, but we were stuck to the floor. When one person did step out, it would not take long before the others followed. During that time, God taught me how to see the anointing oil on someone, to recognize when that person was supposed to be dancing.

Afterward, I would say to that person, "You were supposed to dance." Again and again, they would say, "I know." Then as a group we set up a mutual covering where we agreed that if one was to step out, then the others would too, just to cover that person so the dancer didn't feel all alone. That was fine for a time, when we were still learning to be free. Before going into the service, one dancer would say to the other, "I'll cover you!" Because I knew when dancers were supposed to be dancing, yet they weren't being obedient because of fear, I would sometimes step out and dance right away in order to make the place safer for them to step out.

We struggled with this for about a year or two until I went to a conference where, for the first time, I observed *Christian dance.*

I saw the freedom and the way that the dancers worked together. They danced with tambourines, flags, cloth, swords, ribbons, and anything that could dramatize what was happening in the service. I don't think I closed my eyes once the whole weekend. I stared in amazement, and my spirit leaped as I watched what I knew was the proper way for dance to appear in worship unfold before me.

At the end of the service one night, one of the dancers came and prayed for me and prayed that the chains would come off and that I would be free. I didn't get up and dance right there, but I knew something was done. I went home and that day I called a meeting with all the dancers to explain to them what I had seen. I told them that no more were we going to step back and try to hide, but that now was the time to dance. We took our flags that we hadn't danced with before, and went to church that night and exploded. I don't know what the congregation thought. In the middle of worship, the leader stopped everything and addressed the congregation, telling them that what we were doing was biblical. Then, she continued leading. From that, I assumed there must have been some wide eyes. However, I was free and it did not faze me. We have been dancing ever since. As people began to get hungry for freedom in worship, our team grew from 12 to about 65 at one point.

What I have shared here is my own story—my experiences in the area of introducing dance to a church, but your church will be different. Pray and ask God what to do. Ask for wisdom and advice. You need to know that you are covered by the leadership and released by the pastor. I used to ask the pastor if we could dance behind the people in the balcony, and he would say, "No, I want you at the front where everyone can see you." I thank God for that. Even when I was trying to hide, he wasn't letting me. Because we had this incredible support from our pastor, it paved the way for us to walk in freedom. Go to your pastor and find out where he is with dance. You won't be free in your service until you have his blessing and release.

A Note to Pastors

If you have any questions about dance, I would encourage you to settle them. The congregation knows you and what you think. If you have a problem with dance, so will they. The dancers really need your blessing. Our pastor personally covered us for the first few years because he wanted to really guard us from the questioning and criticism. He didn't grow up in church so he was comfortable with dance. However, I know there was a time when he stood against it, but he changed his mind, took us under his wing, and allowed us to grow and try new things.

If dance is something you really want to see happen and it is a high priority for you, I would encourage you to educate the congregation in that area. You will save yourself many questions and will save the dancers possible problems. Allow the congregation to be a part of what is happening and explain to them the meanings of the colors of the ribbons and flags. This will put some questions to rest and prepare a place for the dancers to be able to move in freedom and release in worship.

A NOTE TO WORSHIP LEADERS

Don't be afraid to use the dancers in a service. If you know that you are doing a song that would be suitable for dance participation, invite the dancers. In my case, when I was leading I sang a song that was about running through the camp and telling the people to get ready. Since I am a dancer, I led the dancers in a processional run around the church. If you yourself aren't a dancer, you can still call on the leader to take the dancers and do something similar. Another thing you can do is request of them a few days beforehand that they prepare something to accompany a certain song.

In addition, if, while you are leading, you are having a hard time pressing into God's presence with the congregation, call on the dancers to come to the front and intercede. You might have hand signals that you use, or you can simply call them verbally. Particularly, if you know you want to have a celebration time, call for the dancers! You will discover that the rest of the congregation will enter celebration more quickly when they see someone leading by example.

CHAPTER 5

Anointing Oils of Dance

FUNCTIONS OF DANCE IN THE SPIRIT

There are different oils of anointing in which a dancer can move. Unction from the Spirit accomplishes each different task. Surprisingly, a person can be anointed in what he or she is doing without having any knowledge of it. The purpose of this book is not to create something in dance that is not there already, but to provide some explanation and language for what may already be happening to (or in) some of you.

Have you ever felt like you wanted to dance over someone while praying for him or her? Have you ever been in a service and had this sudden urge to dance throughout the midst of the whole congregation? Have you felt the Spirit rise up inside of you and you must spin or leap until something is released? These are some of the things dancers have felt.

When such things stir in a person's heart, he or she frequently wonders what is going on. My purpose is to help bring some measure of understanding or assurance concerning these operations of the Spirit.

God has placed gifts within people; all believers should know that. There are different spiritual gifts and different natural gifts. Essentially, anything that can be prayed can also be danced. Just as God has called some to be intercessors, some to be prophetic, some to be worship leaders, so has God called dancers to dance beneath different anointing oils. Here are some of the different anointing manifestations or dance gifts that God has given to different believers. The following list may not be exhaustive but is based on my own observation, study, and experience:

- ❖ Prophetic Dance

- ❖ Warfare Dance

- ❖ Intercession Dance

Prophetic Dance

There are, I believe, prerequisites to moving in prophetic dance—at least for most dancers. Learning to be free in your own personal worship dance, being vulnerable as a dancer, and having a variety of movements to choose from, technically, would be starting places. Sometimes in worship, we aren't being completely honest. Worship then is not entirely real but something put on. If worship is affection toward God then it is only real if we have the affection attached to the action. If we do an action without affection, it is merely action. We need the affection to qualify it as worship. To really communicate something true to a congregation, a person needs to be authentic in his or her worship. To arrive at a mature place in prophetic dance, the dancer must mature. There are qualities and attitudes that can be, and should be, cultivated in the character and life of the dancer.

In order to understand anything, it is best to isolate it from its kindred. What is prophetic dance? How is prophetic dance different from worship dance? Put simply, prophetic dance expresses the heart of God to His people, while worship dance expresses the heart of the people to God.

First, understand that prophetic dance isn't a style of dance—styles may vary. Rather, it involves unction. There are times when God may supernaturally move and you will find yourself moving in response, in ways that you have never done before, but the movements in themselves aren't the prophetic part—the inspiration is.

"Show me prophetic dance."

I had someone say to me once, "Show me prophetic dance." It isn't something that you can isolate or localize in the actual movements. Strictly in point of style, there are different types of prophetic dance. It is best to look at examples:

The first that I want to discuss involves prophetic words incorporated into a dance. In Exodus 15, Miriam the prophetess took up her tambourine and danced and sang a message to Israel (see Exod. 15:20-21). This is a gift of prophecy that is accompanied, and emphasized, by a creative act. Once in a service, I found myself singing a word about allowing the wind to blow. At the same time, I was dancing like wind. This could also happen while someone else was giving a word. One time, someone else was giving a word about God being like an eagle that flutters his wings over his young. As that word was being said, I moved my arms like wings and fluttered them over an area on the floor, acting out what was being said.

The second kind of prophetic dance is one delivered by a group. In a service, God might call your group to do something together; in some cases, He might call your group to choreograph prophetic dance. One dance group, with which I'm familiar, felt that God was telling them to choreograph, and they were wondering if it was God because the church was in a really high time of celebration, but the song the dancers was using was a mourning song. However, they were faithful to work on what God inspired. By the time it was ready, the church had gone through something that took them into a time of mourning. God was using that dance prophetically. Obviously, God knows the end from the beginning. Anything requiring choreography must be inspired beforehand; by its very nature, prior knowledge involves the prophetic—since things yet to come are known only to God.

WARFARE/INTERCESSION

Warfare, as mentioned in the New Testament, is usually talking about a battle that goes on in our minds. The Old Testament involved physical battles. Meditating on these facts can help us better understand why spiritual battles can be fought through the medium of dance.

Instead of simply delivering Israel's enemy over into their hands by force and natural battle, God frequently chose to give them the victory as they praised Him. For this reason, singers, musicians, and dancers lead the way into battle.

In Scripture, we discover that God was very creative in the variety of ways He caused Israel to battle and conquer. For example, Jericho was taken with a shout, not with a weapon. The enemy was taken over as the Israelites walked in obedience to whatever God called them to do.

One of the Hebrew words for dance is *chwul* (Strong's #2342)—to twist, whirl in a circular manner, specifically to travail in pain, tremble, drive away, to bring forth. This has a strong intercessory implication, to drive away and to bring forth! Travailing in pain was what Elijah did when praying for the rain to come. It was what Jesus went through in the Garden of Gethsemane when He sweat drops of blood. A dance carried on in the midst of travail is something full of intercessory power and an act of spiritual warfare. It is like a birth dance. There is work—a calling forth of something in the spirit realm.

We know that prayer can be a powerful intercessory tool, so is intercessory prayer that is danced rather than spoken. There is an authority in the movements God inspires. Dancers may feel something come over them that causes them to dance as though they are driving away and trembling. Such a dance does not look very much like the usual movements of a prima ballerina!

> *The tambourine was used in the Old Testament as an instrument of warfare.*

When God anoints you to intercede in dance, allow your body to move in the manner that He wants. Be obedient to what He is asking you to do. We have studied the use of aids in dance, such as banners. The tambourine was used in the Old Testament as an instrument of warfare. When Israel went into battle, the dancers often used tambourines.

Here are some of the forms of spirit-led dance I've seen in operation:

1. Wall-Breaking Dances: In worship, a congregation can be released and freed into worship through the power and anointing in dance. I term these types of dances wall-breaking dances. Wall-breaking dances are performed when the service is not breaking through to the spirit realm. The dancers go forth in dances of intercession to break down the wall. It isn't a dance that is announced by the worship leader necessarily, but it could be if that were needed. The dancers should be sensitive enough to know when that dance is needed. Remember, these dances have to do with the anointing oil on them, not with the particular moves that are being executed.

2. Dances of Deliverance or Freedom: These dances bring deliverance and freedom to a person. I have seen dancers dance around or over people and the one being danced over in

intercession was set free. It is similar to a wall-breaking dance, but the wall that is being broken down is in a particular person's life. This dance can be performed for an entire congregation as well. In such a case, God calls the dancer to dance through the midst of the people, in order to bring freedom to them in worship or in their lives.

3. Dances of Deep Worship: There are dances that call others to come deep into God's presence. One of my dancers moves in this powerfully, and while she is dancing, I can hardly take my eyes off her. She is anointed to bring people further into God's presence in worship. As I watch, I am eager to see where she is going in worship. She is dancing out of the Holy of Holies. The Holy Spirit is using that dancer to woo the congregation. Something about this dance calls to the worshipers to come a little closer.

4. Dances of Celebration: These dances are usually done in response to joy. In the Old Testament it was done during a festival or a time of celebration. *Chagag* (Strong's #2287) means "to move in a

circle, to observe a festival, to be giddy, celebrate. *Rekad* (Strong's #7540) means "to stamp, spring out wildly for joy, dance, leap, jump, run." Celebratory dance is most often seen in services, as the congregation enters into God's presence with praise! There is something contagious about a joyful dance. As one person is anointed to dance in this unction, it spreads through the congregation until sometimes even the most unlikely people are dancing.

5. Dances of Victory: In First Samuel 18:6, after David slaughtered the Philistines, the women came out of all the cities of Israel dancing and singing. They came out to meet King Saul with a dance of victory. This was done after a battle was won. Have you ever noticed that sometimes after a powerful altar call, if the worship picks up again, there will be more people dancing than there were during the service? This is because there is a victory at the altar that is being celebrated. The people are dancing out of a revelation of the victory they have just reached.

6. Dances of Healing: These can be either to bring about a physical healing or an emotional one. I have seen one dancer who moves in this often and powerfully. She is simply exercising her healing gift and praying in dance. I have seen her dance over people who were very wounded. As a result, they were powerfully touched by God and healed as she danced. Once, in a meeting I attended where there were some people who were sick, one of the dancers there said she felt like she was supposed to dance over them. As she did, they were healed.

7. Dances of Salvation: This dance is anointed to call the unbeliever to God. One pastor's wife told me they were seeing a lot of conversions for a season in their church, and she believed that was directly related to the anointing oil that was on the dancers. Another lady I know said that she feels called to dance with the flags from the different nations and that when she does, she is praying for the salvation of that nation. I believe that this dance will increase as worship is taken out to the streets and into the world.

My husband and I were a part of an outdoor worship time and there were some 75 saved and unsaved people dancing in this market. After it was over, some of the unsaved people there came up to us and told us there was something different about our dance. They said it was free and had life. They invited us out with them afterward, and I believe that it was because they smelled the fragrance of Christ that night through the worship and the dance.

> *My husband is not trained in dance, but dances like a wild man.*

My husband is not trained in dance, but dances like a wild man. We were at an outdoor jazz festival where as far as we knew we were the only Christians there. All of a sudden he turned to me and said, "I feel like dancing!" So he jumped up in the middle of the people and started dancing. I watched as the people who were around whispered and pointed. I could tell that they were drawn to the fact that this person didn't care what anyone thought about him. By the end of the song there was about 15 other people who had gotten up and gathered around and started to dance. It was more than just my husband's dancing that caused those onlookers to join him in dance.

Not all of these types of dances are understood or embraced by the Church. I want to point out here that dance is a form of expression, but dance itself doesn't hold some special anointing unless God chooses to use it. It seems that more and more He is using dance, and ultimately God can use whatever He wants to accomplish something. We just need to be obedient to whatever that may be. The same things can be accomplished as musicians play their instruments in obedience to God. The instruments can be played prophetically, with unction of joy, of intercession, or of deep worship.

In the Old Testament, Saul was tormented by evil spirits. He called David to come and play his harp. When David did so, the evil spirit fled. David was anointed instrumentally to bring deliverance. Dance, and any expression inspired by the Holy Spirit, can accomplish the same purposes.

Dancers, be open to what God may want to do creatively through you. Allow yourself to be used in any way that God chooses.

I have examined some of the dances that you may move in, and there are more I am sure—who can know all that the Spirit of God would do? This isn't to box you in but to help guide you and give you some understanding of what may already be happening to you.

After learning to be real and experiencing levels of freedom in your own dance, then you can go a step further and seek to express the heart of God toward the people. There is a certain call on a dancer's life. God has chosen some to really express His heart to the people. Dancers will have different anointing oils upon them and at different levels will that oil flow!

CHAPTER 6

Worship and Expression

Expression

Creating a dance group and creating worshipers are two different things. Many people can dance and know how to do the moves, but haven't learned to worship. Some haven't submitted their gift to God. Others don't feel called to a freestyle dance in worship, but feel called to do prepared dance, done for other ministry purposes.

We need to consider these matters carefully. Some people will begin to dance, but not really possess the freedom they need in order to minister in the fullest. In my experience, I've discovered that there are two kinds of dancers:

inside-out dancers and outside-in. The inside-out dancers have something inside that they are longing to express and they outwardly demonstrate it. The outside-in dancers know outwardly which emotion is called for and they make themselves adapt to that emotion.

This second type of dancer is able to move in any situation regardless of her personal feelings. That is a positive thing and can be used to an advantage. The negative side to this is that such dancers usually need external direction to express themselves, the lyrics of the song or someone directly telling them what to do.

This approach doesn't allow for freedom in the individual's expression. I believe that most dancers begin by being outside-in dancers. Their goal, however, should be to move to a place where they are dancing from within.

Inside-out dancers don't rely on anything external to trigger expression, but their dance comes from a place deep inside. Not everyone has that inner fountain released, and that is why some individuals are not able to dance in this manner. There may be some serious issues that need to be addressed in order for a particular dancer to grow toward this dynamic. Factors such as shame, fear, self-hatred, a͟ͱ ͟ͻͱ the enemy are all areas that may need to be addressed.

FREEDOM TO WORSHIP

This stage—of moving from external to internal dance motivation—is very important because freedom of expression is a prerequisite to moving in prophetic and intercessory dance.

The same freedom must be obtained by those dancers who are able to express from the inside. Some of the struggles that may need to be overcome though would be ones where the dancer would need to learn how to submit their emotional side to the Spirit in order to lay themselves down and be used by the Lord. Emotional motivation is good, but it is not the goal. Often dancers who do have that internal motivation have a technical weakness and this can be a hindrance. Having a lack of moves is like having a lack of words.

Times devoted to expression are important in creating worshipers. These times will wake up the ability to speak in another language—the non-verbal language of movement! There are many reasons people are not free to express, and there is a process toward freedom that needs to be pursued. I have known dancers who could do all the moves, but when asked to improvise, they simply couldn't. There was no inner working, no inner fountain waiting to pour forth. This is the most important exercise that you can do with your people. If you can bring freedom of expression to someone, you have been a tool in setting that person free forever. That is more important than any dance move you will ever teach them. If you can lead people into expression in worship, their relationship with God will totally change and nothing compares with that. It takes time, exercise, and practice, however, to be able to help people realize their freedom. What you are trying to do is wake up the creativity in the dancers. Some of the things that I have done in order to stimulate this follow:

1. I have the dancers compose a poem about something personal. This in itself may be a challenge to some of them. Once they have written the poem, have them dance it out while someone is reciting it. Following this, take it one step further and have them dance it out, not according to the words, but according to the emotions. When the emotions change, then

the dance should change. Concentrate on the emotional side of the poem here and not the words. This will force them to dance emotionally from within and not outwardly.

2. Take the team to a place in creation where it is really beautiful and ask them to find something in creation that they feel they are like. Then ask them to find something that is similar to the way they dance. Some dancers pick the sun because they want to shine God's glory, and others pick a soft looking lake because they feel that they are soft and peaceful. Some may pick something like a storm because they feel called to dance a dance of warfare.

3. Bring flowers to class, some that are bright and open, and others that are soft and closed. Find as many different and contrasting flowers as you can. Pick out one of the dancers and ask the others to pick which flower they think that dancer is like. Not all will choose the same flower. Go around the room and pick each of the dancers until they all have been compared to a certain

flower. If you have enough and it works out, then give that flower to them.

4. Put on some music that evokes a variety of emotions. Make a list of different emotions that the music expresses and have the dancers make faces that express that emotion. Now ask them to dance out different emotions. As they are dancing, call out different emotions and have them change their dance as the emotions change.

5. Bring some different powders and spices to class (salt, seasoning salt, pepper, coffee whitener, sugar, etc.) Arrange the spices on a table and have everyone at the same time dip their fingers into each one and taste the powder. When they have been tasted, ask around the group to see who they think dances with that taste. Do that for each of the tastes. Then put on music and have them dance out the different tastes as you call them out. (This exercise can also be carried out using different flavors of ice creams.)

6. Ask each dancer to draw a timeline graph of his or her life. The ups and downs of the line reflect the events in the person's life. Once

they are familiar with the pattern of their life-line, have them dance it out.

These are just some sample exercises you can introduce to wake up the feelings inside people. Anything that crosses two expressions or two senses will help to awaken the feeling and expression inside people. For example, taste, smell, then express; touch, see, then express. The point is to dance and write the same emotion or idea. This same crossing of expressions can be applied to other disciplines: to paint and act or to sing and draw the same emotion. Obviously, not everyone is equally comfortable in all of the arts, but it is the emotion behind it that counts, not the resulting artifact or performance. Remember this: if a person worships using every conceivable dance move but isn't free to express what lies within, that person remains trapped.

*Different attacks will
come against all dancers,
and it is up to them
to break through.*

Different attacks will come against all dancers, and it is up to them to break through. It is a process toward freedom, and each dancer will have to fight and conquer. The enemy isn't new in his lies. I have heard the same thing everywhere I go. Even from one side of the world to the next, he attacks with the same things. Here are some of the common struggles. This may help you to detect what is happening when a dancer goes through these.

1. At some time the dancers feel they don't want to step out because everyone is going to think they want attention. Be sure you know for whom you are dancing, and if it's for God, then let nothing stop you!

2. The enemy comes and says that everyone is thinking, "Oh, she's just trying to look spiritual." If you know in your heart that your eyes are on God and that you aren't doing anything for humankind, then you shouldn't be affected by what people think.

3. "You look clumsy!" God doesn't look on the dance moves. He looks on the heart.

4. Intimidation from the congregation or other dancers. Pray for boldness to overcome and force yourself to keep stepping out until timidity is broken.

5. Some dancers are self-conscious, thinking that everyone is looking at them. Probably people are looking and that is part of your ministry—that others would be touched by what you do!

These are just some of the lies that have to be overcome. Freedom comes with a consistent pressing in and seeking after God. Although it becomes easier with maturity, it is perhaps never utterly easy to be up at the front doing things that draw attention to yourself. When each dancer is dancing for the right reasons, each will be covered and dance in a ministering spirit. Freedom comes with knowing who you are in Christ and the call of God on your life. Freedom comes in knowing that Jesus really does want us to worship Him with all our heart, mind, soul, and strength. Freedom comes with confidence in who you are and in freeing the expression that is deep in your heart. Above all, freedom comes when one starts loving Jesus more than one cares about what others

149

think. As long as we care more about humankind's opinion than God's, we will be bound.

These next observations may not apply to everyone. For some, there may come a time when they feel they must emerge into freedom at any cost—emerge with such finality that no one will ever put them back into a box again. When someone becomes free, she feels that she must refuse to allow anything to mar her freedom again. She feels that she will never again allow anything to put her back into bondage. Usually the dancer will come into freedom before the congregation is ready to embrace it simply because, up until that point, the congregation had nothing to accept. Up until that point, their comfort zones weren't being challenged. When a sudden burst of freedom comes, the dancer can't expect everyone to understand. God will teach each one how to be mature in freedom, when to use their freedom and when not to. For example, when you first feel free to dance in a service, you might think, "I don't care what anyone thinks. I am going to dance." That statement is good and is true. There is another side, however, that God is also calling us to remember—love. God calls us to prefer one another in love—not that I am telling you in any way or at any time to compromise what He has called you to do. Simply, be careful not to get bitter and say that your freedom is the most important thing in the world, and everything else has to come second—that if the congregation doesn't understand, that's too bad! Instead, with a right heart, stretch the comfort zones of the people. Give lots of grace to those who are learning.

I want to bring clarity to the difference between a member of the congregation and a dance minister. Anyone can dance, and anyone has the right to dance in a service. In the same way, anyone can sing and has the right to do so at any time. However, not everyone is chosen to sing on the worship team on Sunday morning. Not everyone who plays an instrument is asked to play in the orchestra. There is a different responsibility and call on those who are chosen for such ministry. Those chosen have a responsibility to lead the people into worship. In the Old Testament, certainly in David's time, their equivalent to our *worship team* included musicians, singers, and dancers, all working in harmony. For us to achieve a similar harmony, it is necessary to have a right heart, to be sensitive to the Holy Spirit, and to move with the others who are leading. A congregation member dances because of the presence of God in a service. A dance minister dances to bring the presence of God. That means that whether they feel like it or not, they have a responsibility to move out in what God has called them to do.

A dance minister dances to bring the presence of God.

Just as the worship team doesn't wait for God to move them before playing, so it is with a dancer. They dance to call on God as much as the singers in the worship team. Of course, they will dance because of His presence, but they will not wait until then. In the past, I have over-heard people say, "When God tells me to, then I'll dance." The piano player on the worship team doesn't say, "When God tells me to, then I'll play." It is a musician's job as part of the team that is leading the people. As I said before, anyone can dance; these directives apply only for those chosen to work with the worship teams.

CHAPTER 7

Explaining Your Art

Artists will always have recurring issues with people who are less artistic. One such issue is this: how and when should art be explained? Should it simply be performed or created and left as a puzzle, or should it come with footnotes? Is there room for both approaches? Certainly, when it comes to artistic expression in worship, there is a place to simply express and to be free before the Lord.

There is a sense in which art and creativity exist for their own sakes. We create because we were made to do so. From this view, the artifacts of creativity are their own justification. Creating is part of being a living expression of God—the great Creator! To the mind of a believer, it is obvious that the highest form of creativity is that which is done unto the Lord and for His glory, but there is nothing wrong with just creating for the sake of creating. We create as a response to the fact that we, who are created in the image of God, are creative beings.

If every impulse of art could be explained in plain language then art would be redundant and unnecessary. Artistic expression takes its form as the best or most accessible vehicle for the impulse of the artist. Sometimes there are simply no words for what the artist feels, or if words do exist, they remain unknown to the artist. Even the Spirit of God groans with things too deep for voices to utter in articulate speech .

The creative person finds the need to explain a vexation to others. Why must one explain his or her art? Why always explanations? Why does one need a reason to create, to express? Why does one have to explain the movements that she chooses to use? Why does one need to give a report on the paintings that he paints, the colors that he chooses to use? Why does one need to find some kind of prophetic significance to make the creativity acceptable? Does one need a scriptural reference for putting notes together on the piano or splashing colors together on a page? Why does it all have to *mean* something?

Why does it all have to mean something?

Analogously, you desire to go for a walk. Must that desire be justified? Sometimes you walk with a purpose—for example, to get to the store, or to a friend's house—and sometimes you simply walk for the pleasure of walking!

Do children look for interpretive explanations when they choose their crayons, or their movements when bouncing to beats or swaying to slow music? Do they have to have a reason to play dress up? Do the trees need a reason to grow the way they do? Do the branches need to explain the way they move when the wind blows? Or are they just free to move as the wind blows them? Do the flowers have to give an account for their peculiar dress?

Has not the Master simply chosen to express Himself in a variety of colors though His creation?

Is the water forced to give account for every drop that splashes on the shore? Or does it splash about, racing in joy, or frustration, or sitting in pools still with peace and calm. Does God give us a report as to why He chose to fill the sky with blue and the earth with green? Ironically, these are two colors that some have decided do not match! Do the birds need to give an interpretation for the song that they sing? Or do they just open up their mouths as the sun rises and let the songs come out? Yet all of creation is expressing for Him and to Him; for, as Paul says, "...through Him and to Him are all things: to Him be glory for ever" (Rom. 11:36).

As the psalmist says, "The waters saw You, O God. The waters saw you, they were afraid" (Ps. 77:16). The skies sent out a sound. The clouds poured out water...(Ps. 77:17 KJV). The trees of the field shall clap their hands (Isa. 55:12 KJV). His "lightnings lightened the world...(Ps. 77:18 KJV). The earth is the Lord's, and the fulness thereof; the world, and they that dwell therein" (Ps. 24:1 KJV).

The need to explain art creates a trap—a box. Explaining art is like explaining humor—the process kills the subject! We've devalued art by dissections that are based on fear. One doesn't always have or know a reason for choosing a certain color, movement, note, or beat. The artist just feels it and expresses it. God has hidden Himself in His creation. He didn't send with creation a footnote of explanation—unless one views all of Scripture as that note. In some of creation, such as the deep places of the ocean, or far-off places where humankind doesn't travel, God has hidden Himself. Remember what the Lord said to Job: "Have you entered the springs of the sea? Or walked in the search of the depths?" (Job 38:16). Evidently, God has! These matters seem designed to arouse our curiosity—our desire to discover!

Christ spoke many parables but only explained some of them, leaving others for people to explore and to remain matters of meditation.

ON THE OTHER SIDE

On the other side, however, most congregations, and most people, are not artists. They don't speak the same language that artists speak: for art is a language all its own. Again and again, non-artists have come away from productions, dance shows, musical performances, or art galleries saying, "I don't get it."

The people saying this are only partially correct. Indeed, on a certain level they may very well, *get it!* There is something in the intellect that art bypasses—going straight to spirit, allowing the person to receive, even without the mind, a certain spiritual understanding. Yet, as Paul explains with reference to the mystery of tongues, there is something to be said for explanation of artistic expression.

> *Art is a spiritual expression*
> *that bypasses the mind,*
> *as is speaking in tongues.*

The Bible says that it is better that we prophesy than to speak in tongues because prophecy edifies the body while tongues—when not interpreted—edify only the speaker. I see in this an analogy concerning art. Art is a spiritual expression that bypasses the mind, as is speaking in tongues. It's another language that the spirit understands, but not the mind. It edifies us, but how much more it edifies the whole body when interpreted! The non-artist simply does not speak that language, but it *can* be taught.

Of course, tongues have often been surrounded by controversy. It is the signature of spiritual language to create mysteries while explaining them. It is beyond the scope of this book to explain why tongues exist; I simply appeal to their existence to create an analogy. Understand that the question, "Why does God inspire tongues?" is very much parallel to the question, "Why does God inspire art?"

At The Feast, when we were introducing painting in our worship services (something very new to most of the congregation although not new to us as worship leaders), we decided to teach the congregation how to interpret paintings, to speak that language, and to look deeper into the picture.

We started off by over-explaining. After the worship services, Lora, the painter, would explain every color, every image, every meaning. The congregation loved it. It was something that they understood because they were spoon-fed through it.

As the weeks went by, we explained less and less, and some Sundays Lora would simply say that there was no meaning, only an expression of what she felt. At that point, an interesting thing occurred. There were actually others in the congregation that brought forth meaning that they perceived or felt. It became a body ministry, teaching the people to observe and hear what was being painted.

Eventually, we stopped doing explanations altogether, unless there was something specifically prophetic that Lora wanted to share.

Months later, at a women's meeting with totally different people, I invited Lora to paint. Because we had already gone through the explanation with our local church, I forgot that these women had never seen painting. At the end of the meeting, I discovered that the painting bothered some of the women. They didn't understand it. Some were upset enough that they said they wouldn't come back. Part of me thought, "O well," and another part thought, "I could have actually taken those non-artists by the hand and walked them through the process of understanding, and in the end it would have benefited everyone."

Again, one thinks of Paul, "...I will eat no [meat] lest I make my brother to offend" (1 Cor. 8:13 KJV).

Another example of the difficulties in expression alone as opposed to expression accompanied by explanation arises over the matter of teaching the congregation to appreciate when a dance moves from pure worship expression to something of a more prophetic nature. Expression to God alone needs no explanation: it's for God. Prophecy needs explanation since it's for humankind.

Expression to God alone
needs no explanation: it's for God.
Prophecy needs explanation
since it's for humankind.

If a dancer steps out into a prophetic dance, one way to explain is to dialogue with the congregation after the dance is finished. It would be awkward to walk up to the front and say, "Hi, I have a prophetic dance. Could you all watch now? This is what I'm about to dance, and this is what the movements mean." On the one hand, the dancer may not fully understand. On the other hand, the dance—not the words—is the primary mode of communication the Spirit inspires in the believer. There the explanation should follow the act. The explanation can help the people to understand not only the current prophetic act, but alert the congregation so that the next time they can more readily receive and react to such things.

Many times there is fear in people of what is new. This fact frequently does not allow them to really enter into what God is doing. Yet, we must remember, the Lord says, "I will do a new thing..." (Isa. 43:19). We *must* enter in! Explanation can help to calm people's fears.

Not only does an explanation help the congregation at large, but also it can actually help the artistic believer to better understand his or her own expression—even though the process involves some frustration.

We see, then, that there is a place for explanation for the greater good of the entire congregation, and I would encourage artists who have a hard time with their congregations' understanding of their artistic expression to simply and prayerfully walk them through an explanation. In other settings, no explanation is needed because the people already understand.

My conclusion on whether or not we should explain art is usually that if we just take some time to explain and teach, it will only lead to greater freedom for ourselves in the end. The freer and more educated those around us are, the more they will want to see us express and be free. Some artists don't like explanation. They think it devalues the art. I would rather explain it as much as I can and see an entire church or society become more artistically educated.

Finally, it must be mentioned, sometimes pushing people's comfort zones is a good thing in itself anyway, and to explain would be to take away from the very art itself. Christ frequently performed a prophetic act—such as the Lord's Supper or washing the disciples' feet—and followed the act by offering some explanation as to what He had done (see Matt. 26:26-30; John 13:1-17). On other occasions, such as the mudpack He made for the blind man in John 9, He has left His followers to discover the amazing significance of His acts (see John 9:1-12).

Both sides can be walked, and we should only mark the footprints of our Master and ask Him to direct us, "Here, Lord, should I act and explain? Or should I simply act and let You explain?"

CHAPTER 8

The Arts

Understanding the strengths and weaknesses of the different gifts can help us to recognize and release each other in greater ways. It also helps us to cover one another, for we know where each tends to be weak. This helps us to pray and keep watch over one another. If, for example, we know that the weakness of the evangelist is to compromise and pull away from the Church, then we can walk in close relationship with him or her so that we can help overcome these weaknesses. In general, we can challenge one another and keep one another accountable. Also, knowing that there are appropriate places for each ministry helps to define where we can best feature the

various arts. For example, at The Feast we created a production company called Collective Productions Company
for the evangelistic function of the arts in our community.
Though the leaders of the company were Christians, the
members are not all Christian. Of course, if you are going
to work with unbelievers, you will not be able to require
of them a life of holiness before the Lord—that would be
absurd! Instead, you hope to see change in their lives, but
change wouldn't be a prerequisite for being a part of the
company. In this function, the standard would be different than that of the prophetic ministry within the
Church. The same people whom we would allow to be a
part of the Productions Company wouldn't participate in
the priestly role of the arts in a Sunday service.

FIVE-FOLD MINISTRY AND THE ARTS

I believe it is important to gain an understanding of
how the arts can best function within the framework of a
church in which the five-fold ministerial gifts are recognized and in operation. If believers—and also artistic believers—are given their proper roles, they will be free to
free others. For freedom comes from being what God in-
tended us to be. Ephesians 4:11, where the five-fold gifts

are mentioned, is clearly discussing office gifts, stations of authority, and ministry within the Church. I am referring to the gifts by their function rather than by their office, for a person may well prophesy, for example, without holding the office of prophet. The same holds true for most of the other gifts as well. Therefore, when I discuss a *pastoral artist,* for example, I don't necessarily mean a pastor by official office, but by function toward other believers.

I also want to note before continuing that it is my belief that we are by nature creative and that though we don't all call ourselves artists, we all have levels of creativity inside of us. When I talk about "the artists," I am referring to those who pursue creativity and have a significant level of expression already developed in their lives.

PASTORAL ARTIST

What does the pastoral artist look like? As with any pastor, this person is loving, compassionate, and kind. This person creates a safe place for believers to live and interact. With those who are artistic, this involves providing a safe place for artistic expression. The pastoral artists, due to their need and ability to create, have the capacity to pastor and counsel artists through their emotional ups and

downs, and attempt to release all believers into whatever level of creativity they have inside.

Strengths: People gifted in this manner are all-inclusive, vulnerable, honest, and heartfelt, concerned about the heart of an artist first; they make artists feel good about their artistic journeys; they are encouraging and exhort non-artists to get involved; they are patient and willing to allow people time to grow.

Weaknesses: People gifted in this manner don't always want to take risks with art for fear that others will feel uncomfortable; they have little concern about the quality of art because their focus in on the artist; they are afraid to challenge artists over their technical standards for fear of offending; they don't want to challenge the status quo.

What are they inspired by? People, the love and grace of God, community, and unity inspire them.

Where are they found? In the Church, home groups, participating in the Sunday services.

Idea of freedom: "Perfect love casts out fear" (1 John 4:18). If we could all just love one another, we could all be free to express because no one would be afraid to step out and try something new.

TEACHER ARTIST

What does the teacher artist look like? As with any teacher, this person loves to study and learn; this person is concerned with the quality and professionalism of art, and tends to like history and a biblical basis for art; they are able to help develop artists from one skill level to the next.

Strengths: People gifted in this fashion are strong at teaching, studying, containing information, communicating, and understanding their convictions and beliefs; they are thinkers who often admire detail.

Weaknesses: People gifted in this fashion can be dry and stagnant in their approach, have a hard time leaning on the Spirit of God (leaning instead on facts); they have a hard time saying that a work is finally done; they are highly analytical and can be overly critical of their work and the work of others.

What are they inspired by? Truth, structure, order, process, and student growth inspire them.

Where are they found? Schools of the arts (Youth With A Mission, for example), music stores, dance studios, teaching dance teams or other lessons in the arts.

Idea of freedom: The truth will set us free (see John 8:32). The teacher sees truth as the road to freedom.

EVANGELISTIC ARTIST

What does the evangelistic artist look like? These people tend to be cutting-edge and in touch with where the lost are. They are concerned with art that affects society. They want to see culture moved and shifted by God-filled art. They have a passion for the lost and long to see souls saved, and they like projects that are *big*.

Strengths: People gifted in this fashion are often bold, charismatic, likeable, able to relate to the unsaved; they are bridge builders between the lost and the Church. They are a light in dark places and not afraid to try new things and go places that others might not want to go.

Weaknesses: Instead of being in the world and not of the world, they can tend to be in the world and of the world; they tend to lower their standards and let the darkness affect them instead of dispelling the darkness. They can tend to become bitter and frustrated with the Church; they often feel misunderstood.

What are they inspired by? Souls, big events, the power of God, healing, art that impacts the world, art that is relevant to society as a whole all inspire them.

Where are they found? They are found in the marketplace, coffee shops, art galleries, dance festivals, and pubs.

Idea of freedom: "He whom the Son sets free is free indeed" (see John 8:36). All we need to do is see people saved and set free and they'll walk in their calling—including their creative calls.

PROPHETIC ARTIST

What does the prophetic artist look like? People gifted in this area are confrontational and want to push the boundaries; they push people as well to move into new realms of creativity and of the Spirit. They call people to repentance and are concerned with levels of holiness in the arts. They are challenging; they like to make people feel uncomfortable and like to push them toward God. Their art has an intercessory quality to it.

Strengths: These are people of deep emotion and deep convictions; they can bring people to a place of change and repentance. They carry a burden from the Lord and challenge the status quo. They are black-and-white; they don't care what people think; they are strong.

Weaknesses: They can lack compassion and be impatient; they can be more concerned with truth than the way people feel; their strength of seeing things as black-or-white can create great offense since they are often blunt and harsh.

What are they inspired by? Truth, change, God's Word and heart, the Spirit of God, repentance, the edge, movement and not stagnation inspire them.

Where are they found? People gifted in this fashion are found in churches challenging both the artists and the non-artists with what God is saying. They use their art to communicate their messages. They will also be found in the marketplace pointing out sin for what it is and demanding change.

Idea of freedom: "Where the Spirit of the Lord is there is liberty" (2 Cor. 3:17). They want to connect people with God so that they can find true freedom of expression in the presence of the Lord.

APOSTOLIC ARTIST

What does the apostolic artist look like? People who move in this gift are constantly starting new groups and projects. They have a big picture of the arts and all the roles that need to be filled; they know how to strategically place artists in the right places so that individual artists find the greatest release and freedom. They help beyond their borders: in other churches and organizations, in particular with their arts programs. They can bring artists together for a greater function and are able to draw artists together.

Strengths: These people can see areas of artistic gifting, start and build teams; they are committed to *the big picture*; they provide leadership and covering to the other ministry functions.

Weaknesses: They can be over-workers, controlling, and unconcerned with details.

What are they inspired by? Growth, change, building projects and teams, and seeing people function in their calling all inspire them.

Idea of freedom: "For freedom Christ has set us free. Stand firm, therefore, and do not submit again to a yoke of slavery" (Gal. 5:1 NIV). They will fight to see the artists free and are concerned not just with their own freedom but the freedom of all the artists.

FOUR STAGES OF ART IN THE CHURCH

In my experience, to date, I have observed that there are four stages of development experienced by artists within the Church. Each stage seems to be distinct from the others and necessary for growth. Though we do move back and forth in these stages to some degree, if we are healthy then we will continue to grow and progress through each one. For growth is always toward a definite end; it is not mere, random mutation! It is my hope that you will find yourself able to recognize your own experiences among the things described here. In some cases, this recognition will appear backward, sometimes current, and in some cases—it is my hope and prayer—you will recognize things that are yet to come, so that you may be prepared. Wherever you are in your development, I pray that these observations will bless and help you by helping you to understand the gift of creativity within you!

Stage 1—Beginnings (Artistic Birth)

Scripture tells us not to despise the day of small beginnings (see Zech. 4:10)—the eyes of the Lord rejoice to see a work begin! He makes great things from small seeds—the entire Kingdom of Heaven was created from the single seed of Jesus' death and resurrection.

The process of artistic development begins with self-discovery. When you, as an artist, first recognize that there is a place of creativity within you, and you begin to enter that place, everything is new. Everything is exciting. You find pleasure in everything. Simplicity envelops you. You are not concerned with what people think; you are not even troubled by the level of your talent.

If you have a fairly wide circle of artistic Christian friends, then you can probably name a few people you know who are like this right now. You will recognize them: the dancers who are so excited by every new color of material that they attach to a flag. These are those who work hard to find the right ribbons for their tambourines, create costumes, and are consumed by their new expression! These are the painters who go out and buy all the supplies and try a different painting every night, simply because they are so excited to see what will emerge next when they paint! These are those who are not hindered by the fact that their skill is not as great or as developed as the next artist's. They're just happy to be painting, dancing, and singing!

Every artists has to start somewhere and what better place to start than at that beginning? These are like babies: full of wonder, joy, enthusiasm, and innocence!

Requirements for Stage 1

The only entry requirements for stage one are faith and passion. There is no excellence required—not here. This is the stage where all that the Lord seems to ask of the artists is that they enjoy themselves. It is as if He says, "Go, explore. Find new ways of expressing the life I have put within you."

Transition: Something happens, though, near the end of this stage. There is a dissatisfaction that comes over you, almost an irritation. These are, in fact, spiritual growth pains. I have seen that the process of reaching toward stage two causes much grief for some artists, and if they don't rightly discern the growth occurring, then they will have a hard time indeed. Analogously, it's as if a veil suddenly comes off of their eyes and they realize that there is more out there. They want it. This dissatisfaction, felt in varying degrees, is a necessary phase, for it compels artists to leap forward into stage two!

Stage 2—Growing

I would like to make it clear that these stages are not lockstep; there is latitude and a back-and-forth mobility between them. A child grows out of picture books, but sometimes, out of fondness, takes them down from the shelf to look at them again. Nevertheless, he grows and, as Paul says, puts away childish things (see 1 Cor. 13:11).

Stage two is a difficult stage. It is a place where you realize that there is so much to discover and you want to learn. The task ahead looms larger than the gift in hand; it occupies more of your energy and vision. With this shift in focus comes realization. You realize the limitations of your own artistic achievements. Consequently, an appetite to learn and grow begins to dominate. You want to take classes; you want to interact with other artists. You also want to discover more precisely the nature and level of your own gift.

Perhaps the hardest part of this stage is really the emotions that go along with this change. You feel frustrated and instead of looking happily inward at the fascinating bloom of creativity; your focus becomes outward–fixed on people or things that are "in your way." It is similar to the story of the crippled man who can't get to Jesus. Everyone seems to be little more than an obstacle!

There is a tendency at this point to blame your lack of growth, maturity, and freedom on those around you. Frequently, the main target of this will be the church or church leadership. There comes a desire to be "free" and the level of freedom with which you were content in stage one, now seems like a very small box.

What is really happening is a desire for growth and it is God Himself who is calling you to grow and become more excellent in your talent. You are like a chick hammering at the walls of shell around you! If wrongly discerned, the artist fails to see this as a God-given dissatisfaction and becomes frustrated with his or her surroundings. This is like banging your head on a cupboard door and cursing the cupboard!

During this phase, the artist can become rebellious, bitter, cynical, and selfish. This is not pretty, but—on the other hand—if you never feel dissatisfied, you will never go on to new things!

I have seen another wrestling match occurring in the artists during this stage. Even though they know that there is more, there is also a fear of what that *more* might entail—a fear of the unknown. Did you know that a tortoise can only advance by sticking out its neck? You need to take chances to make advances.

In the pursuit of growth, the artist must overcome this fear and enter into a bigger circle of contemporaries. It is in such settings that the mirror of self-realization may tell you some things that you are not ready to hear.

Let me give you an example. I knew this one dancer who was quite good. She led teams, constructed choreography for events, and danced on worship teams. However, when the desire to learn came over her and she took some classes, she was shocked to find out that she wasn't as good as she had previously thought! She couldn't handle this and quit the classes.

Frankly, in the Church, the level of excellence in the arts is still quite low. As long as you stay within the Church to learn and grow, chances are that you will feel pretty good about your attainments. But the second you come in contact with professional secular teachers, you will have a rude awakening! You will see dancers that are much better than you are. Since the Lord loves the humble heart, this can only be good for you!

Any time you enlarge your circle, in any discipline, you realize that you aren't as good as you thought. When this happens you have a choice. You can push through and learn what you need to—walking in humility and in a teachable spirit. Or you can run back to your smaller circle and surround yourself with the illusion that you are better than you are.

This happened to me, too, when I took classes for the first time. I went from feeling that I was the best, to feeling that I was worst, all in one day. From hero to zero! I had always been the leader and good at what I did–within the circles I frequented. Then on the day I entered a class of adult ballet dancers, I felt as if I couldn't do anything! I was so embarrassed. I dreaded going. I found myself looking for excuses to skip out on lessons. But the real lesson, I couldn't skip.

I had a choice and I made it.

Unlike the girl in the previous story, I stuck it out. I went back again and again. I cried almost every time. I wanted to learn but I was frustrated by my lack of ability. I wanted to blame something other than myself so that I could excuse myself from the grim facts, but eventually I swallowed the pain, stuck it out, and learned!

There is a downside to this growth phase. You feel like you aren't as free as you once were! Personally, at this stage in my growth, I had a strong desire to be freer and to walk in a greater anointing. I thought that I would—that I must—be free at any cost! I looked at Sunday services as the place to gain my freedom and I wasn't going to let anyone stand in my way—very selfish.

But there is an upside to all of this as well. It is usually in the desert of this long stage that you come to an awareness of the nature of your own gifts, freedom, calling, and ability. Though sometimes it is hard to lay hold of, there is a quieting of the soul that occurs as you settle down to walk the road ahead, a peace that descends when you decide that no matter what it takes you in time or effort, you will get there! You will walk this road ahead of you toward the unfolding vision of what God has called you to be.

Requirements for Stage 2

Scripture reminds us that faith and patience inherit the promises (see Heb. 6:12). The Lord requires patience from you during this stage. Let go of your pride and be taught. Remember that we need to be committed to the big picture. For the big picture is the vision of our big God! You won't get there overnight. Persistence becomes an important key. There will be a temptation to quit and not press on through the hard times, but if you refuse to quit, you really will come through to the other side.

Stage 3—Advancing

Stage 3 is what I call Kingdom Art! After enough time sweating it out, hacking your way forward through stage 2, you eventually become comfortable with who you are and what God has called you to be and do. The struggle that was once a scream, filling your inside being, subsides. You calm down and clarity comes. It is in this place of peace that you can now begin moving in a greater maturity in the call on your life. There is an authority that comes and a power that backs up your art. This is the season when people watch you dance and get healed, when the lost see a painting and begin to weep and ask questions about God, when you dance in worship and there is such an anointing that people can't help but be changed, when a note is played that resounds in the Spirit over a city and changes the very atmosphere. The Kingdom of God came near to Jerusalem streets through the mere shadow of Peter; now it comes near through the medium of your art!

This can happen in any stage, but in the first two stages it happens almost in spite of you, and often without your realizing that it is occurring at all. But in stage 3 you wield your sword rather than blindly lashing about.

Stage 3 is also filled with excellence. Your art can stand up on any stage, in the Church, or in the marketplace. Maybe your art always compared favorably to secular art in its content, but now it is comparable in technique and artistry with secular art. There is a level of excellence that causes the world to respect the art as well as the Church.

In music, your band can enter into a local Battle of the Bands and not be booed off of the stage. The dancers can enter into festivals and place in the top three. Painters have their work in secular galleries. Not everyone is called to a secular art ministry—to move his or her art into the marketplace—but this is a big call on the Church, to influence society. Art is a powerful voice in society and for this reason God often moves the artist into that arena.

Whether in the marketplace or not, there is a power in the art during this phase that impacts the people experiencing it. Now not only does the art have excellence but it also has anointing, something that the secular artist will simply lack. Though, of course, sometimes the art of secular artists can be powerfully inspired, but that issue is complex.

This stage involves seeing the Kingdom of God advancing into the Church and beyond: into the streets, coffee shops, studios, and theatres. You are taking truth, like salt, and the presence of God, like light, to your church and society through your art—very exciting!

Requirements for Stage 3

To enter and function in this stage requires humility and boldness. The Lord will require you to be bold in order to take His presence through any door He opens. It will be a scary thing at times, partly because the Church is not yet completely in step with what God is calling artists to be, not able sometimes to release the artists and cover them; consequently, you will often be a bit of a pioneer. There probably are not many examples that you can follow—no template—so you will need to be innovative and bold. At the same time, you must give no opportunity to pride. You must not think, "I am the one, and wisdom dies with me!" Be humble. As the Lord gives you favor, and I have no doubt that He will, remember from whom the gift comes—stay humble!

There is a great temptation in the marketplace. You need to be very secure. You are there to influence them, not to be influenced. Again and again, I have seen artists go into the marketplace and get eaten alive. They hold no standards of holiness and they aren't there to bring light. They're there for many reasons, but they are as likely to be spreading darkness as anything else. Don't fool yourself; playing in a pub doesn't make you a stage 3 artist! One fellow told me that he knew many, what I call *stage 3* artists, who play music in the marketplace, but he wasn't sure where they were with the Lord. I told him that they weren't stage 3 artists in that case. The purpose is to overcome darkness with light, not to flirt with the enemy. They may very well be artists but not in this capacity. So be careful, lest you fall.

Stage 4—Reigning

I am including this last stage by faith; for I believe it's coming. However, I must say that I don't really know any contemporary artists who are indisputably living in this place. Personally, I believe that this is the stage in which some of the Christian Renaissance artists lived. This is where, not only do they take their art into the world, not only can it be compared favorably to the world's art, but where they actually are the leading influence—largely dictating the direction art takes. In this place, whether you are dancing, composing music, or painting the ceiling of the Sistine Chapel, the world is looking to you for direction and inspiration!

Requirements for Stage 4

I am projecting here, but we will need strength: to stand in a dark world, to lead when many are following, to stand against unmatched levels of warfare, and strength to fight the good fight of faith!

It is my contention that Christians should rise to the occasion and shine their creativity into the face of society; yet, they are still retreating and afraid they will be infected by the sin that has captured the world of the arts. It is time we got involved, and in doing so raise the moral standard. Society is getting sick of the immorality it is facing daily. Now is the time for us to make our faces seen, our voices heard, and our words read.

Sometimes, Christians have believed that to excel is wrong because it implies that we are proud and need attention. However, God has gifted and anointed His chosen people to shine forth in a world of darkness. That is what light does—it shines! Romans 9:21 states, "Does not the potter have the power to make one vessel for honor and another for dishonor?" This tells me that He has made some to be honored. We have had such a hide-in-the-corner-of-our-churches mentality that the Church has forgotten it is called to shine; it has forgotten *how* to shine. We should be encouraging those with artistic gifts, for "...if one member is honored, all members rejoice with it" (1 Cor.12:26). He has made us salt and light. Salt speaks about flavor, spiritual spice. The creativity that God has put within us is an aspect of that salt. "You are the salt of the earth... You are the light of the world. A city that is set on a hill cannot be hidden. Nor do they light a lamp and put it under a basket, but on a lampstand, and it gives light to all who are in the house. Let your light so shine before men, that they may see your good works and glorify your Father in heaven." (Matt. 5:13-16).

Christian artists, come out from hiding! The Creator of the universe has chosen to make His dwelling place within you! Let the fire of God ignite the creativity inside of you. Let yourself be seasoned with the fire from God. Many of you are today's prophets, given a creative word from God, a word that Christ wants you to proclaim—to His bride and to the world! Too many Christian artists have been sleeping—sleeping giants for whom the world is waiting! It is time to awaken and put on the garments of the poet, the painter, the dancer, and the actor.

For some reason, we have separated the arts and they have been thought of as more evil than the rest of the world. We haven't encouraged the artists; instead, we have been so afraid for them we have squelched the call on their lives. I heard a pastor once say that artists are the hardest people to pastor because they are such emotional people and have such passion burning inside of them. As hard as they may be to deal with at times, their gifts are missed when they do not function within the Body. It is time to stop the separation of the arts from the Church. The business world or political world is full of sin: greed, dishonesty, and hate. Yet, we don't think it evil if someone enters into a career in these areas. The world is the world, and we can't expect holiness to spring out of sin. What we can do, however, is go and raise the moral standard.

The world is the world,
and we can't expect holiness
to spring out of sin.

We can go and make a difference and we must!

Many of the famous artists in Western Civilization that we admire and study about were Christians: Bach, Milton, Handel, Rembrant, Van Gogh, and Dante. These people were leaders in the arts of their day. The world looked at them with admiration, trying to model themselves after them. During the Renaissance, the arts were explosive, and the Church did what it could to support the artist because the Church understood the power behind art. It understood that the world was listening. Unfortunately, over time things changed and the Church stopped taking care of the artists and honoring their gifts. Once again, fear entered into the heart of the Church. The Church lost its revelation that the artist had a ministry. Therefore, we fell behind. The Church went from leading the way in the arts to following. Where once we set the pace, and the world longed to be like us, we now are cheap imitators of what the world is producing. We have lost our edge, and somewhere we became afraid to take risks. The secular artist should stand in amazement, asking us how we do what we do. Our art has become embarrassing at times. We, the Church of the King of Creativity, should be the most amazingly inspired people on the face of the earth.

I am summarizing the following story from *Last Days* magazine. I think it captures what I am trying to say. Vincent Van Gogh was a preacher's kid whose greatest desire was to follow his father into the ministry. When he was young, Van Gogh was very sensitive and compassionate. Basically, he was a typical church kid, but he didn't fit in with the mold. He was ashamed because of his differences, for in his spare time he would draw. He didn't do well in school; historians conclude that he had dyslexia.

When he matured he became a pastor in a coal mining region. Van Gogh identified quickly with the miners and all that they had to endure. He became so much a part of them in his unselfish service that he began to look like a miner. After a year, some denominational officials passing through decided to visit. Upon seeing him, they exclaimed with strong displeasure that he looked more like a miner than a dignified minister! They decided on the spot that he wasn't capable of properly representing their denomination, even though he was effective in his ministry. He was dismissed and sent home.

He was devastated and never recovered from his disappointment. From there, Van Gogh followed his natural inclination and began to study art. He painted his heart out, but there were few buyers. Just before moving to Paris, he tried to put his past behind him and painted "Still Life With Open Bible, Candlestick, and Novel." In it, the candle is snuffed out. A few years later, in a small village outside of Paris, at 37 years of age, Vincent Van Gogh pulled the trigger of a revolver aimed at his own heart; he committed suicide.

He had wanted to be a pastor. After his death he became famous. Van Gogh is responsible for his own actions, but there are many artists now that feel the same way that he did, that they don't fit.

*It is time for Christians
to take a long look at
their attitude toward
art and artists.*

It is time for Christians to take a long look at their attitude toward art and artists. Are we producing things that honor God? We have allowed such mediocrity in the arts. We follow the world's style of dress, music, and its standards in many ways. Our theatre has disintegrated into short skits put together five minutes before being performed. Painters are afraid that if their work doesn't have a cross in the middle of it that they will be classified as rebellious.

Artists have lost their passion and the Church has lost the artist.

We have forgotten how to pastor the artist, and therefore, the artist has gone elsewhere as a result of judgmental attitudes and lack of acceptance. We have the idea that everything labeled Christian art should in some way be directly related to a Bible story, or have a very obvious message about Christ contained in it.

I am not saying that it's not a good thing to paint a picture of the cross or to write a song about Christ. I am only saying that to insist on these things is very limiting. God has made some to be extreme in their creativity, and for those people, being boxed in is the same as having their creative nature stripped away. You can't box inspiration. I know that there is a concern about holiness in art. Out of the abundance of the heart, the mouth of the artist speaks. To an artist, creating is speaking, and out of a heart that is full of God will come art that is full of God.

I know that when I feel I have something to express, I can't always speak it with my mouth. I might write a poem or a song. If that doesn't say it, then I might paint a picture or draw. I have written entire plays, produced and directed them, just because I have something I am trying to say. Today, still, the Church has often misunderstood famous artists. Frank Peretti took his book *This Present Darkness* to 14 different publishers before someone would sign him on. Why? Because it was different! It was a fantasy! Artists, it is time to step out and let the chains fall off of you so that you can run and be free. Create! Lead the way!

> *As an artist and a dancer,*
> *I want to see excellence brought*
> *back to Christian art.*

As an artist and a dancer, I want to see excellence brought back to Christian art. I want to see the Church setting the pace and the example. As a dance leader, I don't want to model myself after secular dancers, but I want to press on and strive to be excellent in what I do. I realize that not all are called to this, and it would be wrong for some to try and walk that path.

There are those of you who feel that God doesn't want you to be trained. I danced for five years before I felt released to be trained. The anointing of God does not depend on how well you can do the moves. I have had people say to me, "If that is true, then why be trained? If you have one move to dance with, God can anoint that one move." My response: if you have a hundred, He can anoint a hundred!

There comes a time, too, when it seems like you are always repeating yourself in dance and you want more moves. Having some training can open that up for you. However, so can getting on your face and calling out to God to release something new in you. You need to listen to what God is telling you. Much modern choreography is totally unacceptable for Church. However, it can be sifted through and used in teaching. Don't be afraid to do that.

Express what is in your heart to God. Don't let the fear of man stop you from being what you are called to be. Let the sleeping dreams inside awaken; be guided by the Holy Spirit and grow in grace. Freedom in expression is one of the most powerful gifts that an artist can ever possess. Let the caterpillar come out of the cocoon, spread its wings, and become the butterfly that it was meant to be!

Call forth the winds of expression
in your belly to stir and create.

There is a fountain inside that has been locked up and hasn't been moving. The water is stale now from lack of movement. Unlock the wells and draw the water out. Some artists have many wells inside that need unblocking, but regardless of how many wells there are, there is a world and a church out there that is waiting to taste the water that is in your well. They are waiting for your worship song to lead them, your book to teach them, your painting to inspire them. Let the fountains of life be released.

The arts are a doorway to a person's soul. They go past the mind and minister to the deep places of a person's spirit. I believe that God is doing a new thing in the area of the arts and there is a prophetic, evangelistic move in the world of the arts. The windows of worship are opening up and the people of God are finding new ways to express themselves to Him. The arts involve expression and worship involves us expressing our hearts toward God. Therefore, we can use the arts to worship. There is a stirring in the artists, an awakening, a renaissance! There is a deep cry coming from those gifted creatively that isn't settling for a refusal. The whirlwind inside of the artists is causing them to come together and seek for the new. In this coming together, they are finding that many other artists are being stirred in the same way.

The brokenness of the artist can be overwhelming. Because there hasn't always been a place for them, there has been a sense of rejection and a crippling. In the midst of that, some have backslidden, some died inside, and some continued to press on, with ongoing rejection. There has been, on occasion, the safe place where the artist was allowed to bloom. The creative movement is rising and those who have failed to trust God and dream because they were afraid and misunderstood can now come out from their hiding places.

Healing is the artist's bread.

Healing is the artist's bread. As these creative people are coming in touch with what they were made to be, there is a deep sense of misunderstanding and hurt that is surfacing. The first step to an artist's release is an artist's healing. The oil that the Holy Spirit is pouring out right now is an oil of healing and restoration. As this great awakening is coming about, as the sleeping giants are beginning to arise, the need for healing increases.

We are searching. We are desperately looking for a place to go and be accepted in what we do. There is a place. There is a place being created just for you artists. God hasn't forgotten you; He has an ancient room in which all the wines of the ages are stored. Within His people He has placed the taste and time of different wines. When the day comes for that wine's release, the Master of the Vineyard goes into the ancient room and opens up the bottle. As He does, all of that wine that has been stored within His people is also opened up. You have looked for your place, knowing that there wasn't a release for you, a place for you to be poured out. But the Master of the Vineyard knew the wine had to be aged, and so it waited inside of you for the perfect moment of its release. Don't be dismayed, for the Master of the Vineyard has chosen to break this bottle open. So as the glass shatters, the vessel is broken, and the prophetic wine of the artist is outpoured. Your day has come, artist!

Take risks. That isn't easy, but it is necessary if you are ever going to move forward in what God has called you to do. As long as you hide, you won't shine in your fullness because something will be blocking the radiance of who Christ is in you. Will you look back at the end of your life and say that you fulfilled your call?

Grow in strength, in freedom, in wisdom, and in love. Serve God and serve humankind!

OTHER RESOURCES BY HEATHER CLARK

Heather Clark Live From Lakeland:
For the First Time

ISBN: 0875531003703 CD $17.99

Additional copies of this book and other
book titles from DESTINY IMAGE are
available at your local bookstore.

Call toll-free: 1-800-722-6774.

Send a request for a catalog to:

Destiny Image® Publishers, Inc.
P.O. Box 310
Shippensburg, PA 17257-0310

*"Speaking to the Purposes of God for This
Generation and for the Generations to Come."*

**For a complete list of our titles,
visit us at www.destinyimage.com**